2-

MORE
JAPANESE
GARNISHES

YUKIKO AND BOB HAYDOCK

MORE JAPANESE GARNISHES

HOLT, RINEHART AND WINSTON · NEW YORK

Copyright © 1983 by Robert and Yukiko Haydock
Foreword copyright © 1983 by Shizuo Tsuji
All rights reserved, including the right to reproduce
this book or portions thereof in any form.
Published by Holt, Rinehart and Winston,
383 Madison Avenue, New York, New York 10017.
Published simultaneously in Canada by
Holt, Rinehart and Winston of Canada, Limited.

Library of Congress Cataloging in Publication Data
Haydock, Yukiko.
More Japanese garnishes.
1. Cookery (Garnishes)   2. Cookery, Japanese.
I. Haydock, Bob.   II. Title.
TX652.H 944   1982   641.8   82-1556
ISBN 0-03-063611-6

First Edition

Illustrations and photographs by Bob Haydock
Design by Amy Hill

Printed in the United States of America
10 9 8 7 6 5 4 3 2 1

CONTENTS

Color plates appear between pages viii and ix and between pages 78 and 79.

FOREWORD

The desire to decorate is a human trait. It probably did not take man very long to progress from simply satisfying the basic human needs for food, clothing, and shelter to the desire to make those things more beautiful. In the matter of food, we have gone far beyond the stage of eating merely to fulfill a need. We have devised different ways to prepare food, crafted dishes to serve it in, and learned to decorate the finished meal.

It is only natural that such decoration would reflect one's culture. One of the special characteristics of Japanese cuisine is that when it is served it should reflect a feeling of the seasons. It is also essential that the chef become a master at his craft. Part of that craft is the technique of carving and cutting, which developed rapidly during the Edo period and which symbolized the flowering of the townspeople's culture.

We Japanese do not seek beauty in size or grandeur. Rather, we are attracted to small things and unimposing presentation. We like to see infinite space in small, self-contained units. In the traditional art of flower arrangement the artist will discard all but a few essential flowers in order to create his small universe. One also sees quiet and simple elegance in the tea ceremony. The desire is to submerge oneself in the tranquillity that remains after all unessentials have been discarded.

Mukimono has its origins in that cultural background. It is interesting that the Japanese tradition of decoration has gone in just the opposite direction from that of the West. In the West, especially in France, table and food decoration made great progress between the sixteenth and nineteenth centuries, culminating in the colossal pièce montée. It is surprising to compare pièce montée to Mukimono. One is astonished at the wide disparity between the two desires to "decorate food." Bob and Yukiko Haydock's charming book is an intriguing effort to unite these two cultural traditions in a quiet search for beauty.

—SHIZUO TSUJI
Tsuji Professional Culinary Institute, Osaka, Japan
Author of *Japanese Cooking: A Simple Art*

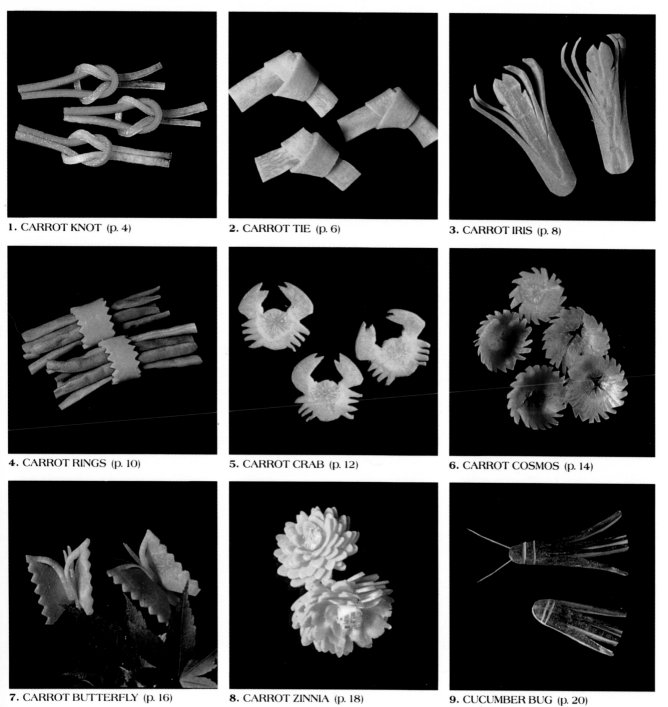

1. CARROT KNOT (p. 4)

2. CARROT TIE (p. 6)

3. CARROT IRIS (p. 8)

4. CARROT RINGS (p. 10)

5. CARROT CRAB (p. 12)

6. CARROT COSMOS (p. 14)

7. CARROT BUTTERFLY (p. 16)

8. CARROT ZINNIA (p. 18)

9. CUCUMBER BUG (p. 20)

10. JAWS (p. 22)

11. WASABI BOAT (p. 24)

12. PINE TREE (p. 26)

13. CUCUMBER SAILBOAT (p. 28)

14. CUCUMBER BUCKET (p. 30)

15. CUCUMBER FLOWER (p. 32)

16. CUCUMBER FAN (p. 34)

17. CUCUMBER LEAF (p. 36)

18. EGG CHICKS (p. 38)

19. EGG CAR (p. 40)

20. INSIDE-OUT EGG (p. 42)

21. EGG PLUM BLOSSOM (p. 44)

22. QUAIL EGG CHERRIES (p. 46)

23. ORANGE MUMS (p. 48)

24. ORANGE BASKETS (p. 50)

25. ORANGE TULIPS (p. 52)

26. ORANGE RABBITS (p. 54)

27. TOMATO FLOWER (p. 56)

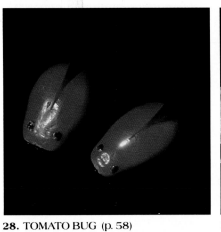

28. TOMATO BUG (p. 58)

29. TOMATO DAHLIA (p. 60)

30. MAGNOLIA BLOSSOM (p. 62)

31. TURNIP CUP (p. 64)

32. DAIKON MUM (p. 66)

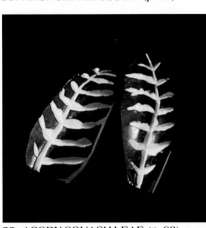

33. ACORN SQUASH LEAF (p. 68)

34. LILY BULB ROSE (p. 70)

35. LOTUS BALLS (p. 72)

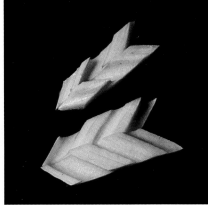

36. LOTUS ARROW (p. 74)

INTRODUCTION

Our first book, *Japanese Garnishes: The Ancient Art of Muki-mono*, was introduced a few months before publication with a slide presentation at the 30th Annual International Design Conference at Aspen in June 1980.

It might seem strange that the introduction should be before a group of designers and architects rather than cooks. But, in truth, no audience could have been more suitable. The Japanese, probably more than any other people, have made art part of life and food part of art.

Long periods of peace and prosperity are required for a culture to develop fine cuisine with embellishments such as Mukimono. The Japanese had both during the well-known Edo period (1603–1867) when the powerful Tokugawa clan achieved supreme power under Ieyasu. They began a 250-year era of peace and isolation that permitted many of the arts we admire today to develop and flourish. Mukimono came into its own during this time. It is interesting that it is flourishing again today when Japan, after coming through some difficult years, is once more beginning a new era of success and well-being.

We have been grateful for the many letters that were sent to let us know how much the first book was enjoyed. We hope this one will be as happily received. As in *Japanese Garnishes*, we have tried to select only the simplest garnishes. The simple cut or slice that transforms food is the true art of Mukimono; ornateness is seldom satisfying or appropriate.

For this new volume, we have added a concluding section of recipes. Mukimono, after all, is only part of the whole, and we thought we should put it back in context.

Finally, we are grateful to the many good friends, both here and in Japan, who have helped us with these books. Our special thanks must go to Seiji and Yaeko Nakagawa, our dear friends in Kyoto, Japan, who have patiently helped us during many trips to their beautiful city; to Shizuo Tsuji, author of *Japanese Cooking: A Simple Art*—our admiration for his work led us to ask him to write the foreword to this book, and to our delight he graciously accepted; to Kiichiro Imanaka, owner of

Kansai Restaurant in San Francisco, who promised to help us with everything we wanted to know and proved more than equal to the task; to Toshiro Kandagawa, well-known Osaka restaurateur and television chef, who spent many hours showing us the "food capital" of Japan; to Mataichi Mashita of Kyoto, who dazzled us with his Mukimono artistry; to Hitoshi Morimoto, Chairman of the Board of Directors, Daikyo Kansai Chefs' Association in Tokyo, who has been very kind; and finally to our longtime San Francisco friends Shigetaka and Fumiko Suzuki, owners of Sanppo, a superb Japanese restaurant in San Francisco, to whom we first went for advice when we were undecided about doing the original book. They have faithfully offered us encouragement and help ever since.

GARNISHES

TOOLS

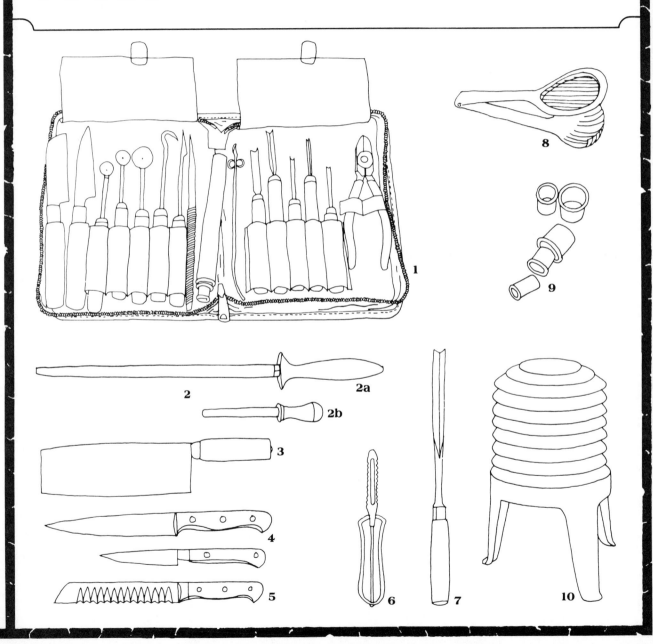

In all skills tools are important, and Mukimono is no exception. The illustration shows all the tools you will need. For the most part, the garnishes don't require unusual tools. Ordinary kitchen paring knives will usually suffice.

1. THE MUKIMONO SET. In Japan it is possible to buy a set of Mukimono tools, which usually come in a zippered leather case. The price ranges from slightly under $100 to many hundreds of dollars, depending on the assortment and quality. The set shown is about $100. A set like this isn't necessary for the garnishes in this book, but for the cook who has everything . . .

2. KNIFE SHARPENERS. The first rule in using knives is always keep them sharp. The classic way to accomplish this is with the sharpening steel (2a), a round, tapered hard-chromed steel bar with a handle and hilt usually about 20 inches long overall. The small Zip-Zap ceramic sharpener (2b) is also a good choice. Since it is only about 5½ inches long it can be kept handy.

3. JAPANESE CHEF'S KNIFE. This shouldn't be confused with a cleaver (which it might resemble in the drawing). It is actually quite lightweight and has a thin blade. It is very useful in making the peeling cut, as in the Daikon Mum (see page 66).

4. PARING KNIVES. Most garnishes can be made with these conventional kitchen knives.

They are relatively inexpensive so it pays to buy good ones. One with a 4- to 5-inch blade and one with a 2- to 3-inch blade will be useful.

5. GARNISH KNIFE. This knife has a blade that zigzags from left to right. A potato cut in half with this knife will have a ribbed surface.

6. VEGETABLE PEELER. This is one of the most familiar kitchen gadgets and has yet to be improved upon.

7. V-SHAPED CHISEL. This is not a cooking shop item. For this you will have to visit your local hardware store. We use one 8½ inches long with a ¼-inch V.

8. EGG SLICER. This is also a familiar item. Taut wires are strung across the cutting area to neatly and evenly slice a hard-boiled egg.

9. GARNISH CUTTERS. These come in many sizes, designs, and prices. We recommend the less expensive ones. In this book we use only the circular cutters, but a variety is nice to have.

10. PEEL 'N EGG. This is brand-new and is the best way that we have ever found to peel an egg quickly and cleanly. The top and bottom of the egg are broken to let air in. The egg is placed over the hole in the upper part. The cover is put on, and a sharp downward pressure of the hands pops the peeled egg out the bottom. PEEL 'N EGG, Woebbeking Mfg., Inc., Glen Flora, Wisconsin 54526.

3

CARROT KNOT

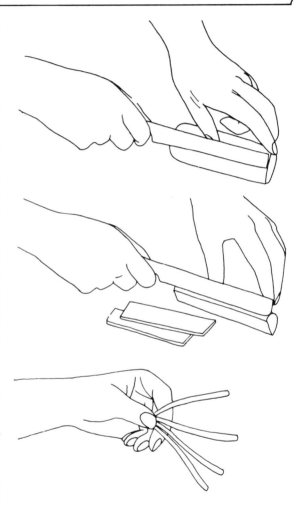

When a gift is given in Japan, a special decorative string called mizuhiki is often used to tie the parcel. This is one of the knots that is traditionally used. So this garnish could symbolize your wish to give your guest the gift of a fine meal. Please note that this garnish can also be made with a parsley stem. See color plate 1.

SERVING SUGGESTIONS: Use in a green salad or with broiled fish.

YOU WILL NEED: carrot, Japanese daikon, Japanese chef's knife, bowl of salt solution.

1. Cut a carrot into strips 6 inches by ³⁄₁₆ inch by ³⁄₁₆ inch. If you want to mix orange and white colors as we have done, also cut a piece of Japanese daikon into strips the same size.

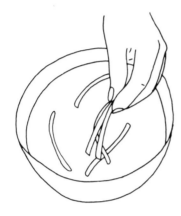

2. The strips should be soaked in salt solution (1 tablespoon salt, 1 quart water) until pliable.

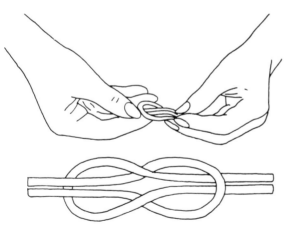

3. Tie the knot as shown in the diagram. It is probably easiest to make one loop and weave the other into it. Rinse with cold clear water to desalt.

CARROT TIE

Those of you who have been to Japan have probably noticed that most shrines have a tree to which visitors tie little pieces of paper, each containing a written wish. The paper is folded lengthwise several times and tied with this knot. So we might say the garnish symbolizes a wish for a tasty meal. See color plate 2.

SERVING SUGGESTIONS: Use with potato salad or coleslaw.

YOU WILL NEED: carrot, Japanese chef's knife, bowl of salt solution.

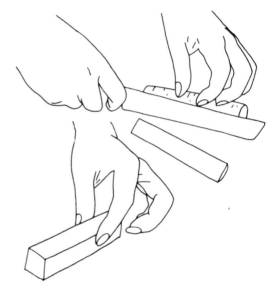

1. Cut a 5-by-½-inch block from a carrot.

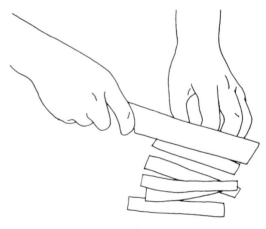

2. Slice the block into thin strips (5 inches by ½ inch by ⅒ inch).

3. Soak the strips in salt solution (1 table-spoon salt, 1 quart water) until pliable.

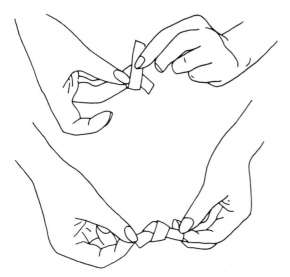

4. Make the tie as shown. Rinse with cold water to desalt.

CARROT IRIS

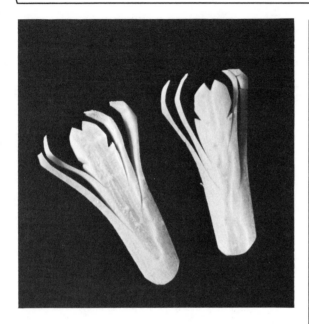

The principle here is to cut a block into an interesting shape and then slice off the garnishes—Mukimono mass production. You needn't restrict yourself to the Carrot Iris shape. Experiment. See color plate 3.

SERVING SUGGESTIONS: Use on a green salad or on a sandwich plate.

YOU WILL NEED: carrot, thin-bladed knife, bowl of cold water.

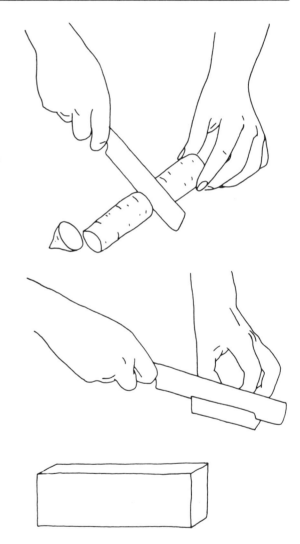

1. Cut a 3-by-¾-by-½-inch block from a carrot.

3. Slice the block into garnishes. Soak in cold water to make them crispy.

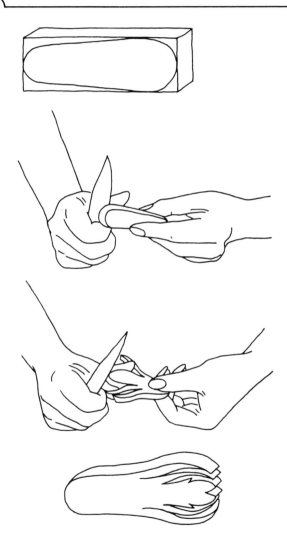

2. Shape the block into the flower form, as shown.

CARROT RINGS

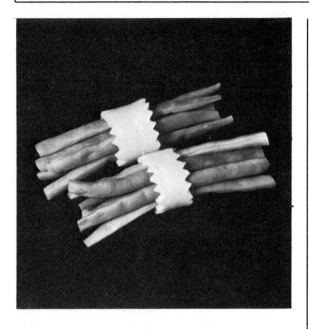

In Japanese cuisine, vegetables are often tied together in nice little bundles. Unfortunately, many of the roots and vegetables used for tying are not available here. The Carrot Ring is an attractive alternative. See color plate 4.

SERVING SUGGESTIONS: Use as a way of presenting string beans or asparagus in an appealing, different way. Note instruction number 5 when cooking.

YOU WILL NEED: carrot, vegetable peeler, knife, V-shaped chisel, cylindrical garnish cutter.

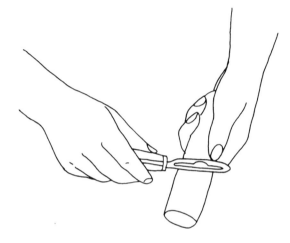

1. Peel a fresh carrot with a vegetable peeler.

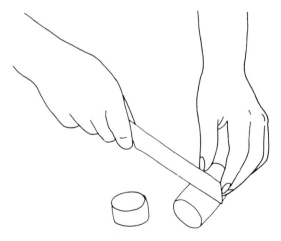

2. Cut into cylinders.

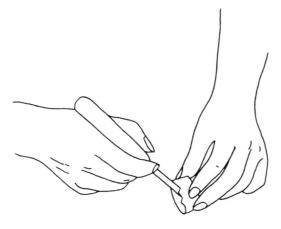

3. Notch the edges with a V-shaped chisel.

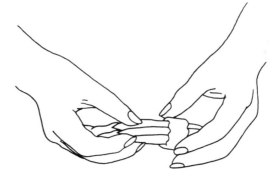

5. Insert the string beans and cook until just done. To preserve the vivid green color, do not cover the pot while cooking.

4. Cut out the centers with a circular garnish cutter.

CARROT CRAB

The Carrot Crab is another example of carving a block into a shape and then slicing off the garnishes. It is a fast way to do many garnishes and invites a lot of creativity. Try flowers, birds, animals, or just abstract shapes. See color plate 5.

SERVING SUGGESTIONS: Cook in boiling water for about two minutes and float on a serving of crab bisque.

YOU WILL NEED: carrot, sharp thin-bladed knife, pot of salted water.

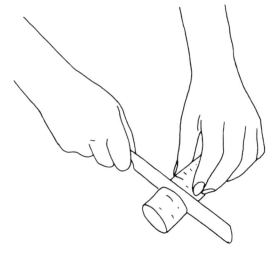

1. Cut a 1-inch or 1½-inch section from a fresh carrot.

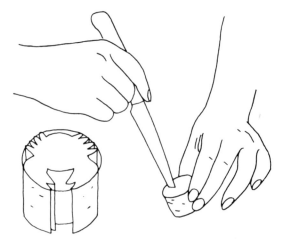

2. Shape the piece, as shown.

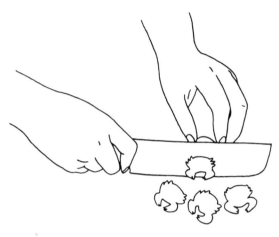

3. Cut into crab garnishes. Drop in lightly salted boiling water (1 teaspoon salt, 2 cups water) until just done or the garnishes turn a bright orange.

CARROT COSMOS

These garnishes are easy to make once you get used to the peeling cut. This is not a straight slice, but an angled cut that preserves the cone shape. This gives each garnish a three-dimensional quality. See color plate 6.

SERVING SUGGESTIONS: Use on or around escabeche of sole or potato salad.

YOU WILL NEED: carrot, vegetable peeler, pot of cold water, a small knife. (If you have a small flat Japanese Mukimono knife it would help.)

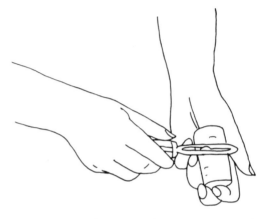

1. Cut a 3-inch section from a carrot and peel with a vegetable peeler.

2. Shape the block, as shown, by notching the edges and forming a slight cone shape.

14

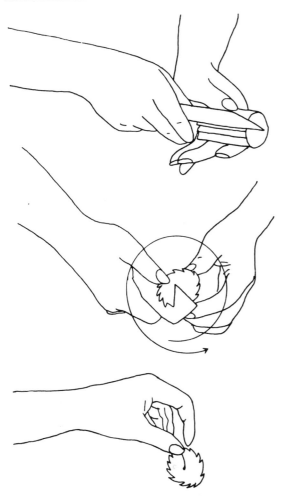

3. Slice off the garnishes from the cone-shaped end with a peeling motion, preserving the cone shape. Make slightly more than a 360-degree slice. Soak in cold water for crispiness.

CARROT BUTTERFLY

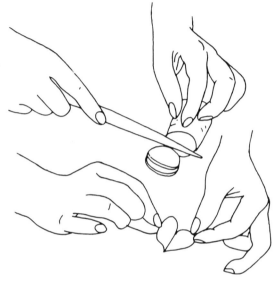

This is a garnish that everyone should try. It is not hard to do and is truly delightful. Instead of slicing the carrot straight down, which makes a circular slice, you might try a more oval cut. This will produce a much longer butterfly with longer antennae. Also, you can angle the garnish knife cut more. See color plate 7.

SERVING SUGGESTIONS: Use on top of boiled artichokes or on chicken aspic.

YOU WILL NEED: carrot, paring knife, garnish knife, pot of cold water.

1. Make a thin ⅛-inch slice about three-quarters of the way through a peeled carrot. Then make a second slice completely through. This creates a slice with two halves, as shown.

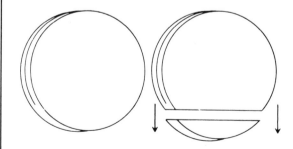

2. Slice the bottom, being careful to cut low enough so that the two sides remain attached.

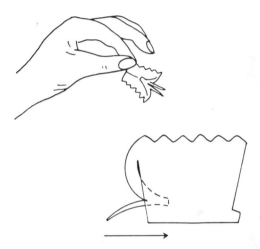

4. Insert the head section between the two wings. Soak in cold water to open wings fully.

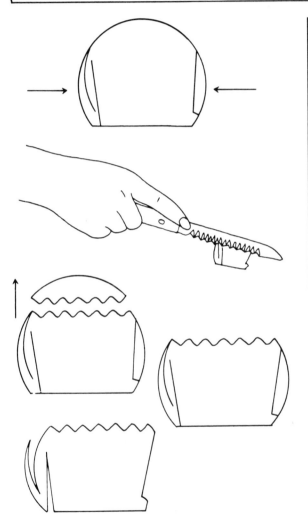

3. Make the cuts in the body, as shown. Then cut off the top with a garnish knife, creating a jagged cut.

CARROT ZINNIA

The Japanese raise some giant carrots that are almost 2 feet long. They also raise some tiny ones about 3 inches long. Too bad we can't get the giant ninjin here. We could make really large, beautiful Carrot Zinnias. Nevertheless, try to find the fattest carrot you can for the larger petals and graduate downward. See color plate 8.

SERVING SUGGESTIONS: Place around a platter of sliced cold turkey, alternating with Cucumber Leaves (see p. 36).

YOU WILL NEED: carrot, cucumber, thin-bladed knife, toothpick, pot of cold water.

1. Cut a 3- or 4-inch carrot cylinder and shape it so that one end is smaller. This tapered shape is to give different size petals. You may also use two cylinders from the thick and thin parts of the carrot.

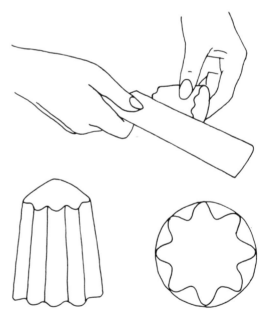

2. Make grooves around the sides and cut the small end to a cone shape.

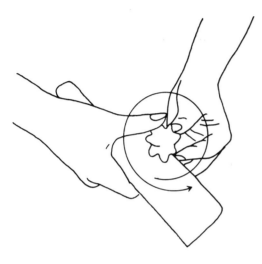

3. Slice the petals from the cone end with a peeling motion, preserving the cone shape. Cut slightly more than a complete circle.

4. Make the center of the zinnia out of a small piece of cucumber. Score a design in the green skin. Insert a piece of toothpick.

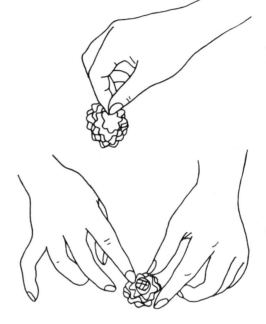

5. Assemble the petals from large to small. Attach them to the cucumber centerpiece. Soak in cold water.

CUCUMBER BUG

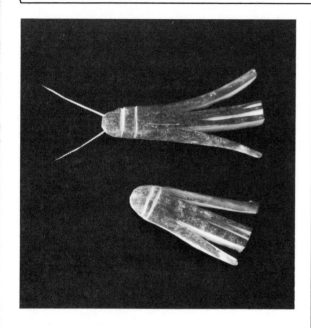

We can't promise that your guests will remain as cool as cucumbers when they find this little fellow in their salad, but we suggest you try him out anyway . . . he's seedless, burpless, and nonbitter! See color plate 9.

SERVING SUGGESTIONS: By all means make a few of these for your next picnic lunch. Nothing wrong with bringing your own bugs.

YOU WILL NEED: cucumber, pine needles, paring knife, pot of cold water.

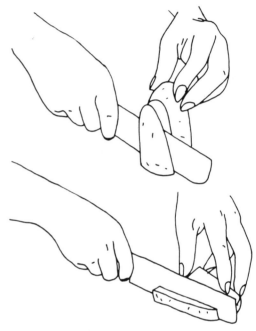

1. Cut a small section from a cucumber, about 2½ inches by ½ inch.

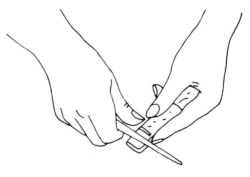

2. Score the lines across the head.

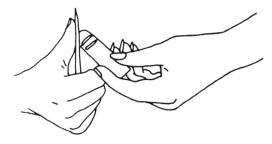

3. Round the head slightly.

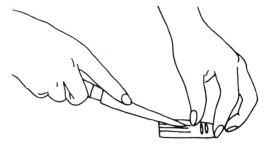

4. Make the slices for the wings.

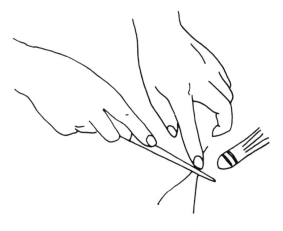

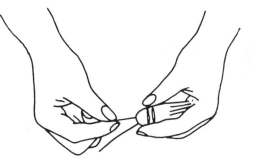

5. We are using pine needles for the antennae. Cut them to size and insert them in the head. Soak in cold water to open wings.

JAWS

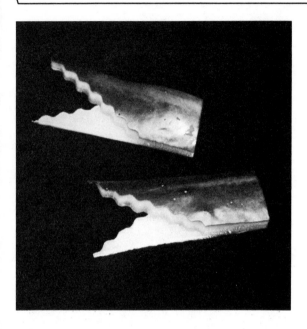

Actually, Jaws is not the Japanese name for this garnish—unless they have changed it recently. It is called kiri-chigai, which really refers to the type of opposing diagonal cuts that are used. See color plate 10.

SERVING SUGGESTIONS: Is it too much to suggest serving this with seafood?

YOU WILL NEED: cucumber, Japanese chef's knife, garnish knife, bowl of cold water.

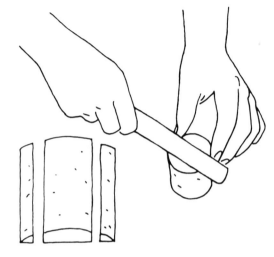

1. Cut a small section from a cucumber, about ¾ inch by 2 inches.

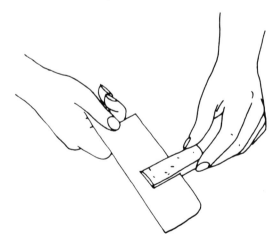

2. Insert a Japanese chef's knife down the center as shown. Skin side should be up.

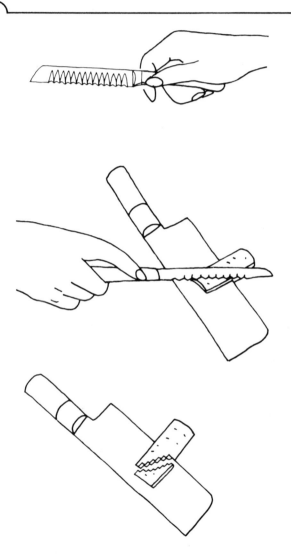

3. Using a garnish knife, make a diagonal cut to create the "jaws" on one side.

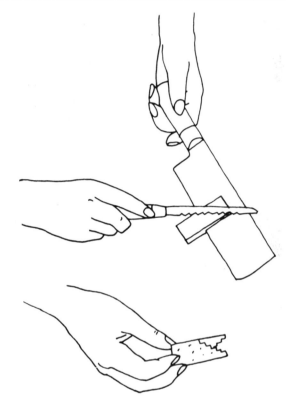

4. Turn the blade over and cut the "jaws" on the other side. Put in cold water to keep crispy.

WASABI BOAT

In Japanese cuisine, small containers like this are made to hold wasabi, the green Japanese horseradish. They are known as wasabi dai. This is a simple oval shape that presents the wasabi very nicely. See color plate 11.

SERVING SUGGESTIONS: Use these boats for serving wasabi with sashimi. Use for horseradish with a roast beef or tongue sandwich.

YOU WILL NEED: cucumber, Japanese chef's knife, paring knife, toothpick.

1. Remove the skin from the end section of a cucumber by cutting away an egg-shaped slice. The slice should not be flat, but should follow the curvature of the cucumber.

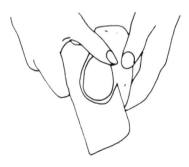

2. Cut another slice. Try to retain the curving spoonlike shape.

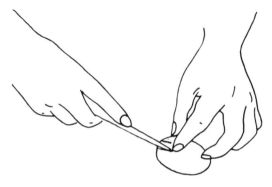

3. Make two ¾-inch slits at the large end of the slice.

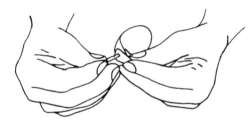

4. Overlap the three sections and pin with a piece of toothpick.

PINE TREE

This is an elegant garnish. Although quite simple to make, once it is made, most people can't quite figure out how it was done. Everyone is charmed with it, however. See color plate 12.

SERVING SUGGESTIONS: Use with escabeche of scallops, tomato salad, or salmon mousse.

YOU WILL NEED: cucumber, Japanese chef's knife or paring knife.

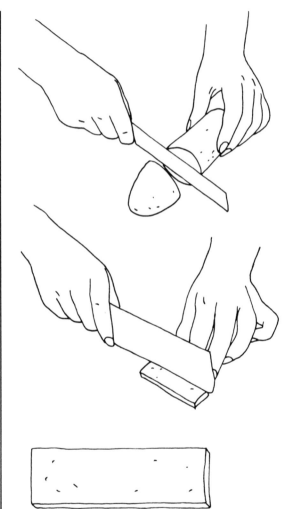

1. Cut a 3-by-¾-by-¼-inch piece from a cucumber, as shown. (Use Japanese or pickling cucumbers, if available.)

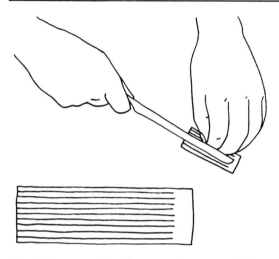

2. Cut many thin slices to about ¼ inch from the end.

3. Now, with a sharp knife, make shallow angled cuts across these slices.

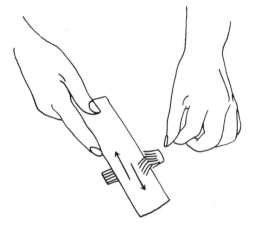

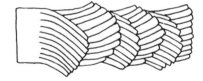

4. As one cut is made push the "pine needles" to the right. On the next cut push them to the left, forming the garnish as you go.

CUCUMBER SAILBOAT

This is another fun garnish for light occasions that is fairly easy to make. The garnish should be cut from the stem end, rather than the flower end, of the cucumber since there are fewer seeds at that end. See color plate 13.

SERVING SUGGESTIONS: Serve along with a cucumber sandwich.

YOU WILL NEED: cucumber, Japanese chef's knife, toothpick.

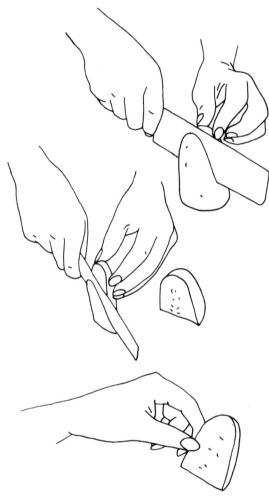

1. Cut a slice about 3 inches long from the stem end of a small cucumber. (Use Japanese or pickling cucumbers, if available.) The slice should be about ⅜ inch thick and include the curved end.

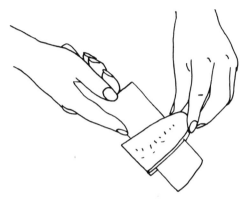

2. Create the sail by slicing horizontally to about ¾ inch from the curved end.

4. Prop up the sail by using a toothpick for a mast.

3. Shape the stern end.

CUCUMBER BUCKET

There seem to be more cucumber garnishes than any other kind. Perhaps because the cucumber has been around for centuries, there has been more time to practice on them. In this case, the Japanese turn the old-timer into a tiny bamboo bucket to contain small culinary delicacies. See color plate 14.

SERVING SUGGESTIONS: Use for seafood cocktail.

YOU WILL NEED: cucumber, Japanese chef's knife, spoon, toothpick, yakitori stick.

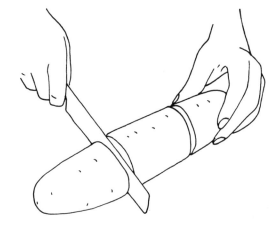

1. Cut a 3-inch cylinder from a cucumber.

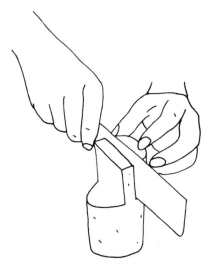

2. Cut off the excess on each side of the handle.

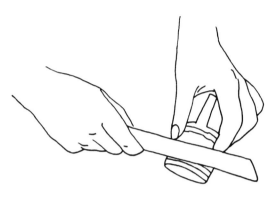

3. Carve the design into the body. We are using a bamboo design, but it's fun to try different patterns.

5. We are using a bamboo yakitori skewer for the stick.

4. Shape the handles and neatly scoop out the insides with a spoon. Insert the crosspiece, which can be cut from a scrap of cucumber and secured with short toothpick pieces.

CUCUMBER FLOWER

The Cucumber Flower is a good example of how a simple twist or cut can transform a vegetable into an interesting garnish. Here the twist creates a nice three-dimensional shape out of an otherwise flat slice. See color plate 15.

SERVING SUGGESTIONS: Use it to surround a caviar mousse or to garnish slices of smoked salmon.

YOU WILL NEED: cucumber, thin-bladed knife, V-shaped chisel, bowl of cold water.

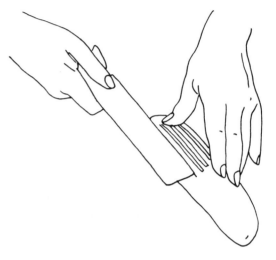

1. Using a knife or V-shaped chisel, cut shallow V-shaped grooves into the skin of a cucumber, going completely around the circumference.

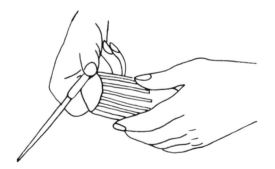

2. Cut off the end and shape it into a cone.

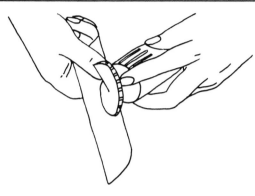

3. Slice off the garnish, making three revolutions. Keep the slices fairly thin, about ⅛ inch.

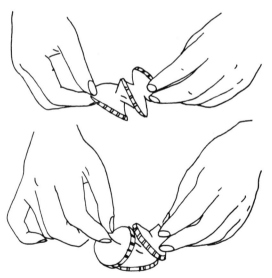

4. The two outer slices can be twisted under to support each other and form the three-dimensional shape. Drop in cold water to keep them crisp.

CUCUMBER FAN

Simplicity is usually best. Here a multitude of slices will transform an uninteresting piece of cucumber into a delicate fan. It is graceful, simple, and very typical of the best in Mukimono. See color plate 16.

SERVING SUGGESTIONS: Use with a shrimp salad.

YOU WILL NEED: cucumber, sharp thin-bladed paring knife.

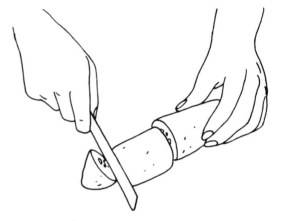

1. Cut a 3-inch cylinder from a cucumber.

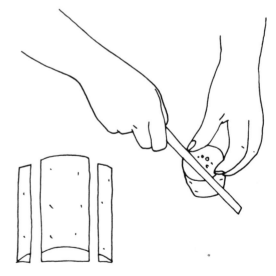

2. Cut the shape as shown (3 inches by ¾ inch by ½ inch).

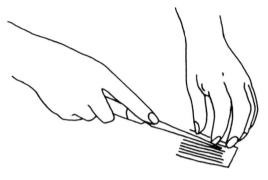

3. Make many thin slices to about ½ inch from the end.

4. Fan out the slices by pushing down with the finger at the joint end.

CUCUMBER LEAF

The Cucumber Leaf is a variation of the preceding garnish in that a series of thin slices are used to transform the cucumber into a graceful shape. In this case, the result is a leaflike garnish that is elegant enough for the most formal dinners. See color plate 17.

SERVING SUGGESTIONS: Serve with broiled fish.

YOU WILL NEED: cucumber, thin-bladed knife, chopsticks.

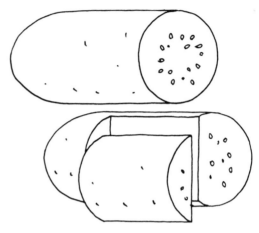

1. Cut a 3-inch section of a cucumber, as shown.

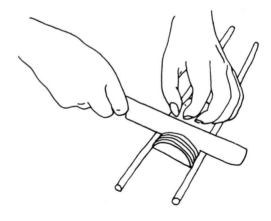

2. Make many thin slices across the entire length. Use two chopsticks as a guide to prevent cutting all the way through.

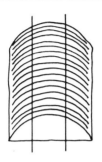

3. Cut the center piece so that it is about 3 inches by ¾ inch.

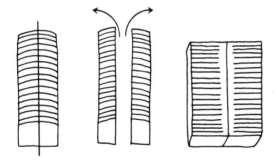

4. Cut this piece in half lengthwise and turn the halves outward so that they are on their sides.

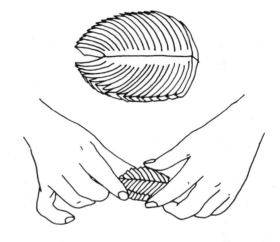

5. Bring the two halves together and fan in the shape of a leaf.

EGG CHICKS

In making egg garnishes it is important not to damage the white when peeling the shell. The best device we have found for this is PEEL 'N EGG (see p. 3 for address). If you haven't used one of these, by all means try to get one. You'll be amazed. See color plate 18.

SERVING SUGGESTIONS: Of course, Egg Chicks are a natural for a children's party.

YOU WILL NEED: egg, bits of carrot and raisin, PEEL 'N EGG, small paring knife.

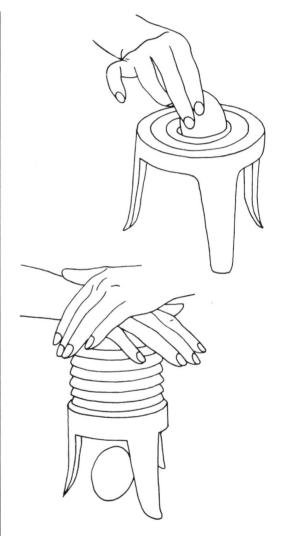

1. Carefully peel a hard-boiled egg so as not to damage the white.

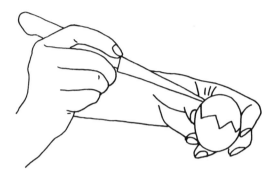

2. Make the diagonal cuts around one end, as shown.

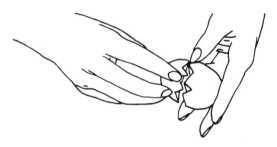

3. Remove the top. This should expose the yolk.

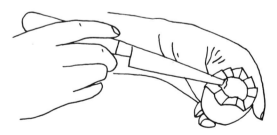

4. Carefully clean up the loose pieces of egg white.

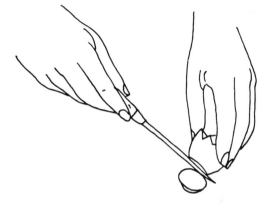

5. Cut off the bottom to act as a base.

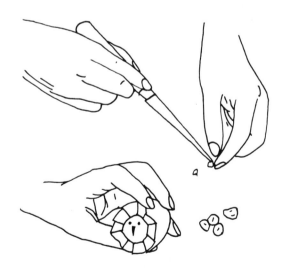

6. The face can be made from bits of carrot and raisin.

EGG CAR

The Egg Car is another garnish for children. With that in mind, you should be careful to use little bits of celery rather than toothpicks to attach the wheels. As soon as the child realizes the Egg Car doesn't roll very well he will probably just eat it, so we want to be careful. See color plate 19.

SERVING SUGGESTIONS: Make them for a children's party, of course.

YOU WILL NEED: egg, carrot, celery, knife, PEEL 'N EGG.

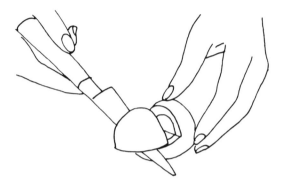

1. Peel a hard-boiled egg and remove the right-angle section, as shown.

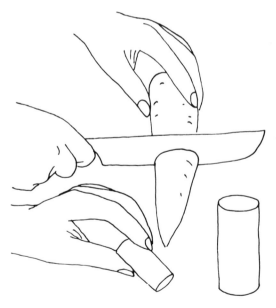

2. Shape a cylinder about 3 inches by ¾ inch from a carrot.

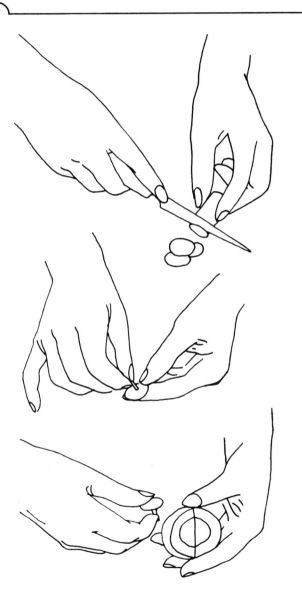

3. Cut the wheels and steering wheel from this cylinder. These are attached with pieces of celery, as shown. The steering wheel should be made slightly smaller than the wheels.

INSIDE·OUT EGG

Only the Japanese could ever think of this kind of garnish. The white is where the yolk is supposed to be and vice versa. If you like to fool Mother Nature, then try this one. A warning, though: this is probably the hardest garnish in the book to do. Mother Nature is tough! See color plate 20.

SERVING SUGGESTIONS: You might put a slice or two on top of a chicken salad sandwich. Wherever you use it, you won't want it to go unnoticed; it's too hard to make.

YOU WILL NEED: eggs, carrot, small knife, spoon, two bowls, pot, egg cup, egg slicer.

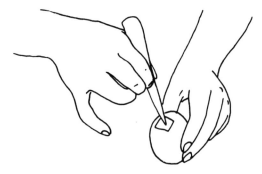

1. With a small knife, tap out a hole in the large end of a raw egg about ½ inch square.

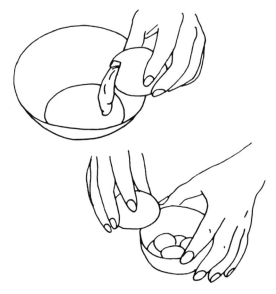

2. Pour the white into one container and the yolk into another. Separate one more egg into yolk and white.

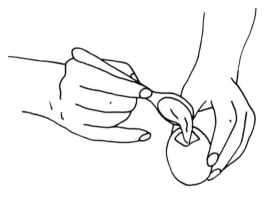

3. Stir the yolks. Spoon the yolks back into the empty shell to about three-quarters full.

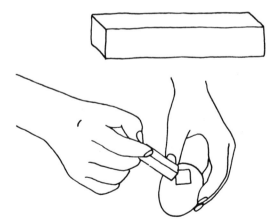

4. Cut a piece of carrot about 3 inches by ½ inch by ½ inch. Insert the carrot into the yolk-filled eggshell through the square hole. The liquid yolks should completely fill the eggshell at this point.

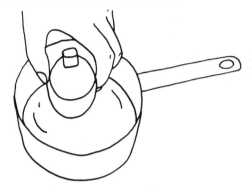

5. Place the egg in an egg cup or other support, and steam until hard, about 10 minutes.
6. Remove the carrot and fill the cavity with egg whites. Steam 7 more minutes or until hard.

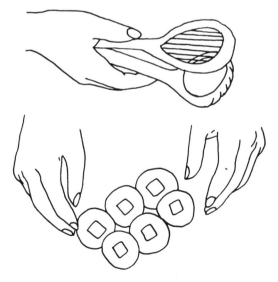

7. Peel, and slice with an egg slicer.

EGG PLUM BLOSSOM

This is a charming egg garnish that is based on the idea that a warm egg can be molded into a new shape. This is also a hard one to do, mainly because eggs are so fragile. But try it anyway, it's worth it. See color plate 21.

SERVING SUGGESTIONS: Use them to top a spinach salad.

YOU WILL NEED: potato, egg, five round chopsticks, PEEL 'N EGG, rubber band, egg slicer.

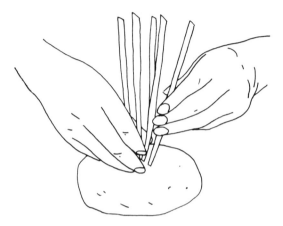

1. Stick five round chopsticks into a potato, as shown.

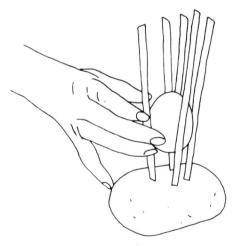

2. Hard-boil an egg and peel while still warm. Insert the warm egg between the chopsticks.

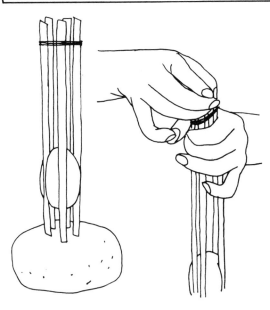

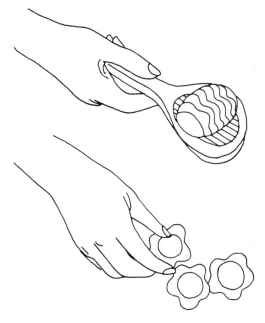

3. Hold the top of the chopsticks together with a rubber band. Allow the egg to cool. The grooves made by the chopsticks will remain in the cool egg.

4. Remove the egg and cut into slices with an egg slicer.

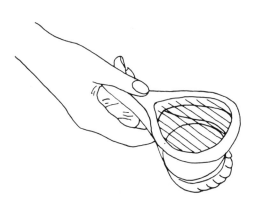

QUAIL EGG CHERRIES

The delightful thing about quail eggs is their size—about the same as a big red cherry, which is obviously the inspiration for this garnish. The Japanese were the first to cultivate wild quail for the purpose of obtaining the eggs, which are now available in some Oriental markets here. See color plate 22.

SERVING SUGGESTIONS: The eggs will dye to a rich bright red, so they are marvelous for colorful accents on an hors d'oeuvres or sandwich tray.

YOU WILL NEED: quail eggs, red food coloring, bowl, pine needle or other stem.

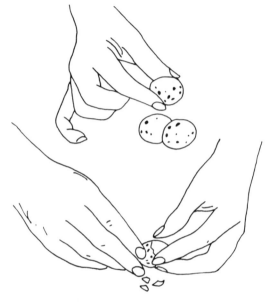

1. Hard-boil and peel several quail eggs.

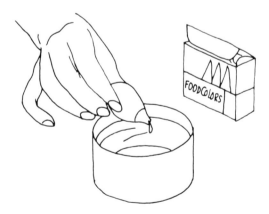

2. Prepare the red food coloring.

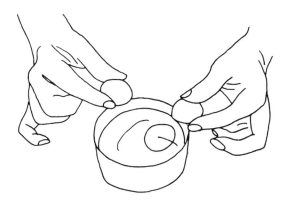

3. Immerse the eggs and leave them until dyed to a rich bright color.

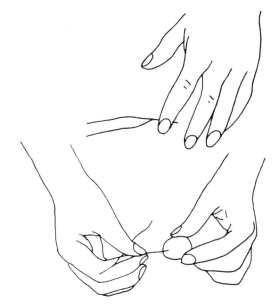

4. Insert pine needles for the stems.

ORANGE MUMS

Again, simplicity is the key. This regular pattern of cuts is all that is needed to make an ordinary orange half into something a little special. See color plate 23.

SERVING SUGGESTIONS: Orange Mums can be used to garnish duck à l'orange or fruit salad.

YOU WILL NEED: orange, sharp paring knife.

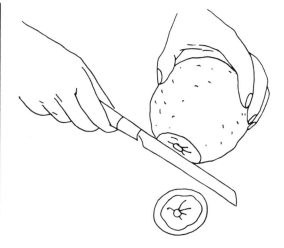

1. Cut both ends off an orange.

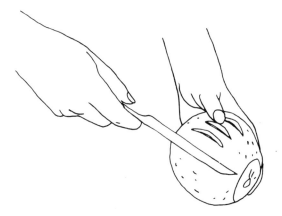

2. Using a sharp knife, cut 2-inch-long notches around the circumference. The notches can be cut through to the meat.

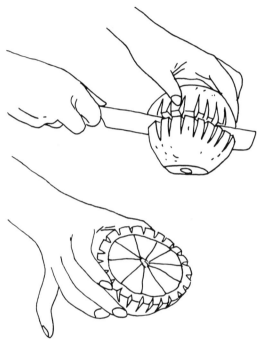

3. Cut the orange in half. The halves will rest on their flat bases.

ORANGE BASKETS

Container-type garnishes usually delight guests and are useful besides. The orange is a natural container, and lots of interesting things have been done with it. We have chosen two ideas that we especially like. See color plate 24.

SERVING SUGGESTIONS: We are serving mandarin oranges in one, cranberry sauce in the other. Both would be bright complements to a roast turkey.

YOU WILL NEED: orange, paring knife, grapefruit knife, ribbon.

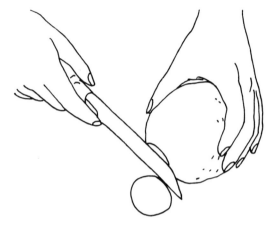

1. Cut both ends from an orange.

2. Slice the orange in half.

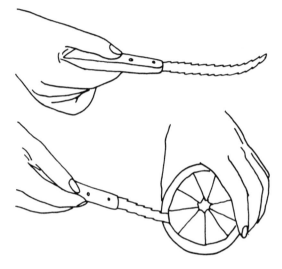

3. Using a grapefruit knife, remove the meat.

4. Cut the skin almost halfway through on each side for the handles.

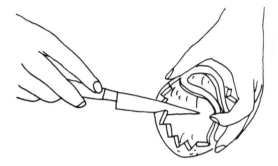

5. Cut the design along the edge.

6. Tie the handles with a nice bright ribbon.

ORANGE TULIPS

Orange Tulips are our second orange container. In choosing oranges at the market, the thicker-skinned ones are probably best, as they will hold their shape better. See color plate 25.

SERVING SUGGESTIONS: We have added a scoop of sherbet to turn it into a dessert treat.

YOU WILL NEED: orange, paring knife, grapefruit knife, ice cream scoop, sherbet.

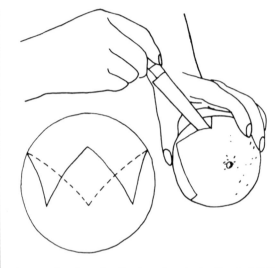

1. Make the six diagonal cuts in the orange as shown, cutting through to the center. Try to make all cuts equal in length.

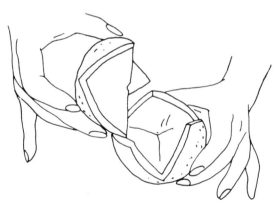

2. Separate the halves.

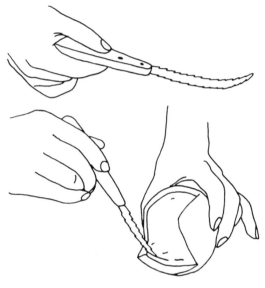

3. Remove the meat with a grapefruit knife.

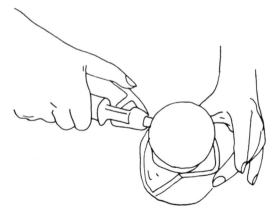

4. Fill with a scoop of orange sherbet.

ORANGE RABBITS

God gave bunny rabbits big ears so that children and Mukimono chefs would find it easy to make them. This is a fine rabbit garnish that any child or Mukimono chef would be proud to call his or her own. See color plate 26.

SERVING SUGGESTIONS: These can be quite nice garnishing duck à l'orange, or perhaps a pork dish or fruit salad.

YOU WILL NEED: orange, knife.

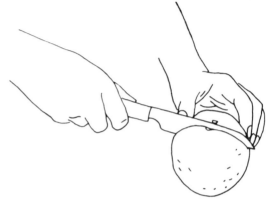

1. Slice an orange in half at the stem.

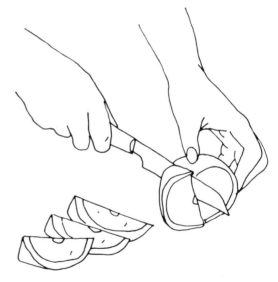

2. Cut into six wedges.

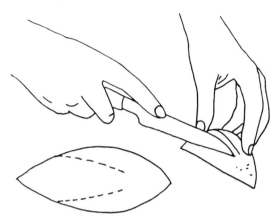

3. Make the two cuts shown through to the meat.

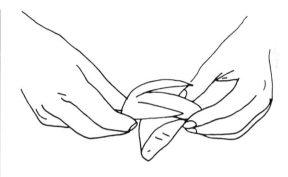

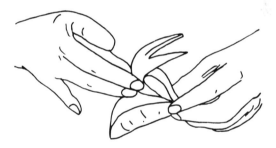

5. Wedge the tip of the skin back underneath itself so that the "ears" remain erect.

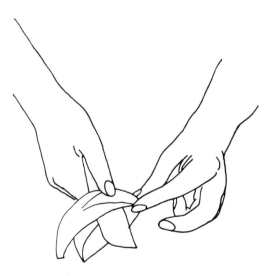

4. Slice the skin away from the meat.

TOMATO FLOWER

In the United States, tomatoes weren't considered food until about the 1850s. It is said that they were only grown as decorative plants. If so, the early Americans could have used a few Japanese tomato garnishes. Well, better late than never, here are three of our favorites. See color plate 27.

SERVING SUGGESTIONS: Use with roasts, in the center of a celery root salad, or on a cheese tray to add color.

YOU WILL NEED: tomato, paring knife.

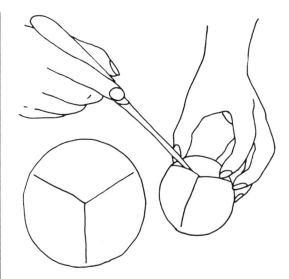

1. Cut through the skin in thirds, as shown. Be careful not to cut through to the center.

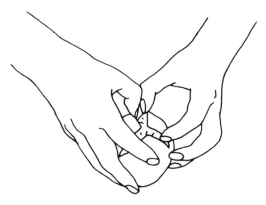

2. Carefully open the tomato.

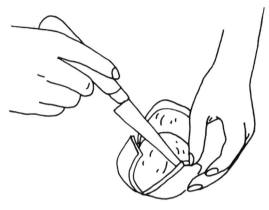

3. Cut away the fiber connecting the sides to the meat. Try to retain the ball shape of the meat.

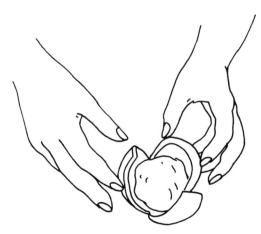

4. When all of the connecting tissue is cut the tomato will remain open.

TOMATO BUG

For centuries the tomato has been a staple in Italian cooking, especially the Italian plum tomato. This is a small pear-shaped tomato that is prized for its meatiness. We prize it for its shape, which with a couple of simple cuts and peppercorns for eyes becomes a cute little red creature. See color plate 28.

SERVING SUGGESTIONS: Use alongside a Spanish omelet.

YOU WILL NEED: Italian plum tomato, paring knife, peppercorns or cloves.

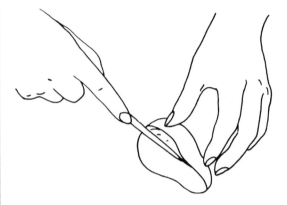

1. Cut an Italian plum tomato in half.

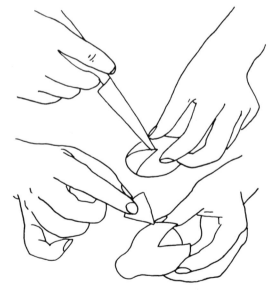

2. Cut and remove the tail piece.

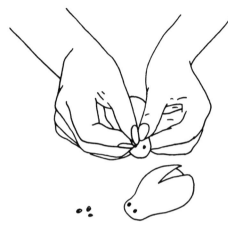

3. Insert peppercorns or cloves for the eyes.

TOMATO DAHLIA

In our first book on Japanese garnishes we included the Tomato Rose, which is made out of a long slice of tomato skin. It is a beautiful garnish and is quite well known. The Tomato Dahlia is similar, but not seen as often. It is done with simple straight cuts into the tomato and looks very dramatic. See color plate 29.

SERVING SUGGESTIONS: Surround with stuffed eggs or use with a pork or veal roast.

YOU WILL NEED: tomato, knife, spoon, lettuce or leaves for the nest.

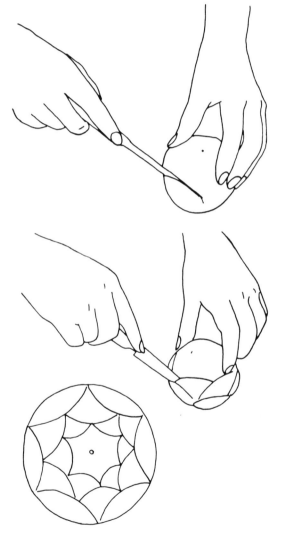

1. Cut a tomato in the pattern shown.

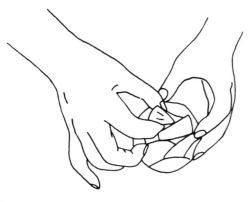

2. Remove the center with your fingers.

3. Spread the petals out.

4. Add a dollop of mayonnaise or other dressing in the center, and arrange on lettuce or other leaves.

MAGNOLIA BLOSSOM

The eggplant was first farmed in China and India. It was later introduced into Turkey, Greece, Spain, and Italy, and eventually was brought to the New World by Spanish explorers. The eggplant we need for the Magnolia Blossom, however, is the smaller elongated Japanese eggplant (nasu), which is now available in California and elsewhere. See color plate 30.

SERVING SUGGESTIONS: Arrange several with green leaves as a centerpiece for the buffet table.

YOU WILL NEED: 2 Japanese eggplants (one slightly larger), carrot, small knife, V-shaped chisel, cold water, lemon juice, toothpick.

1. Select two Japanese eggplants. Remove the stem and leaves completely from the smaller one. On the other leave a short stem and trim the leaves so they are attractive.

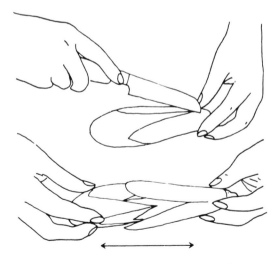

2. Cut each eggplant into three petals.

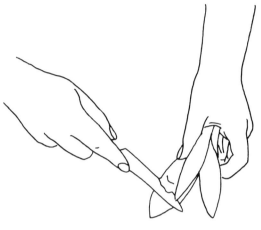

3. Scrape away most of the inside pulp to produce attractive petals. Rub lemon juice on cut areas.

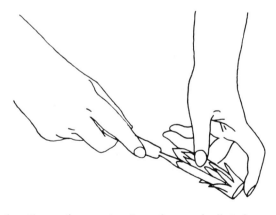

4. Carve the centerpiece from a bullet-shaped piece of carrot with a V-shaped chisel by shaving slivers all around. Soak in cold water to open.

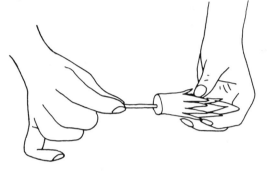

5. Insert a toothpick in the bottom of the carrot.

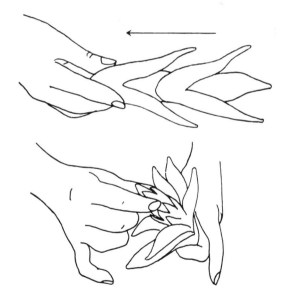

6. Insert the stemless eggplant into the other one. Leaves should not overlap. Pin together with the carrot centerpiece. Soak in cold water to keep crisp.

TURNIP CUP

The trick to this garnish is to cut five equal sides. When a skilled Mukimono chef does it—rapidly and without measuring—*they are equal!* The sides have to be equal or the garnish will look lopsided. Fortunately, when we do it we can take more time and measure. See color plate 31.

SERVING SUGGESTIONS: Use as a cup for wasabi or hot mustard.

YOU WILL NEED: turnip, knife, Mukimono scoop or small spoon, bowl of cold water.

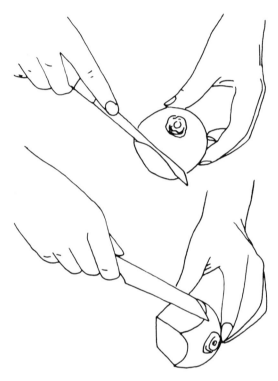

1. Shape a turnip into a pentagon.

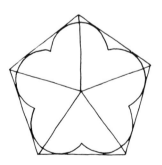

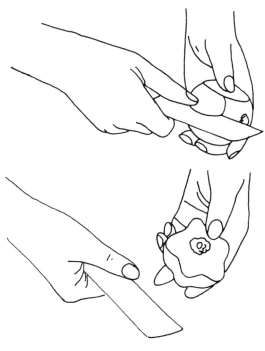

2. Round off the pentagon's corners.

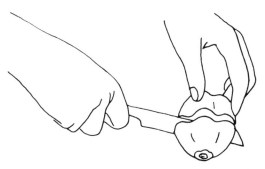

3. Slice off the top third of the turnip.

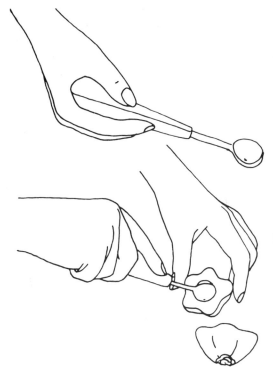

4. Scoop out a small cavity in the center. We are using a scoop from a set of Japanese Mukimono tools, but any small spoon will do. Immerse in cold water until ready to use.

DAIKON MUM

The flower garnishes are probably the most impressive in Mukimono. Some chefs will produce elaborate bouquets. The Daikon Mum is a good example. It also shows how easily a rather complicated-looking garnish can be made. See color plate 32.

SERVING SUGGESTIONS: Several can be used as the centerpiece for a buffet.

YOU WILL NEED: Japanese daikon, carrot, chefs knife, bowl of salt solution, toothpick, bowl of cold water.

1. Cut a 4-inch cylinder from a Japanese daikon.

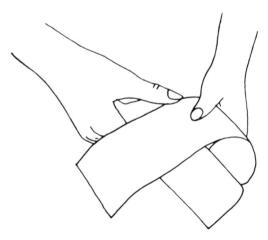

2. Using a peeling cut, make a flat piece about 7 inches long.

3. Soak in salt solution (1 tablespoon salt, 1 quart water) for about 5 minutes, or until pliable.

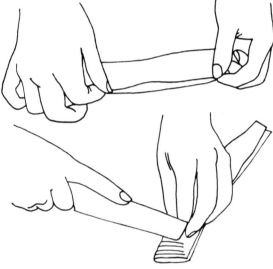

4. Fold over lengthwise. Make a series of 1½-inch cuts about ⅜ inch apart for the full length of the strip.

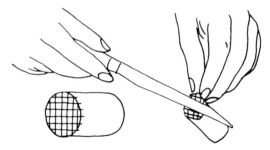

5. Cut a ½-inch-diameter cylinder about 2 inches long from a carrot. Cut a crisscross pattern in the end as shown.

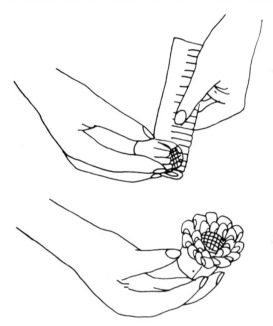

6. Roll the carrot up inside the daikon, and pin with a toothpick. Soak in cold water to make it open nicely.

ACORN SQUASH LEAF

The acorn squash is a hard-shelled, small squash that is also called the table queen, Danish, or Des Moines squash. It has a rich blackish green skin that covers an orange flesh. When a design is cut into the skin it is quite striking. See color plate 33.

SERVING SUGGESTIONS: Cook in seasoned broth and serve with a roast or baked ham.

YOU WILL NEED: acorn squash, Japanese chef's knife, V-shaped chisel, cooking broth.

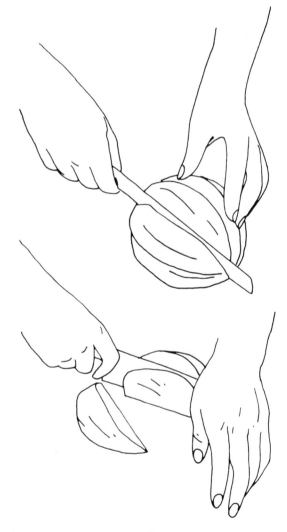

1. Cut an acorn squash into sections, as shown.

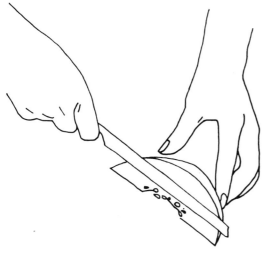

2. Cut away the seed portion.

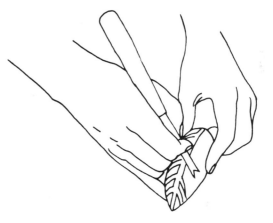

3. Carve the pattern in the skin with a V-shaped chisel. Cook in your favorite seasoned broth until just done.

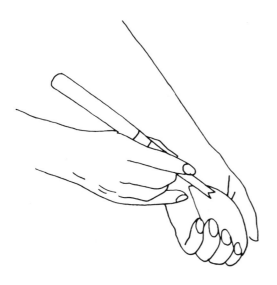

LILY BULB ROSE

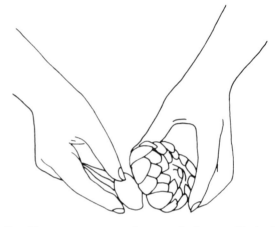

1. Remove unattractive petals from a lily bulb until a pleasing, regular shape is obtained.

The lily bulb (yuri-ne) is abundant in the winter in Japan. The bulb is always parboiled before eating to remove its bitterness, and is most often used in steamed dishes, soups, or salads. Next Easter, after your potted lily dies, its bulb can live on as a garnish. See color plate 34.

SERVING SUGGESTIONS: Use to garnish a buffet tray.

YOU WILL NEED: lily bulb, knife.

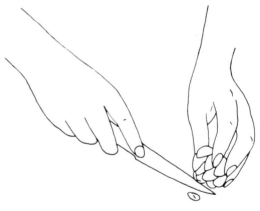

2. Cut away the tip.

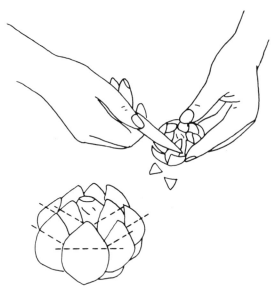

3. Cut off the tips of the petals all the way around.

LOTUS BALLS

The lotus root is distinctive because of the hollow tubes that run through it. By cutting in different ways, many designs are possible. However, lotus root discolors, so Fruit-Fresh (available in grocery stores) should be used soon after cutting. Rubbing lemon juice on the lotus root will also prevent discoloration, though it imparts a taste as well. When buying lotus root, beware of soft spots, which indicate that the inside is discolored. See color plate 35.

SERVING SUGGESTIONS: Use several on an hors d'oeuvres tray. Try dyeing them different colors.

YOU WILL NEED: lotus root, knife, Fruit-Fresh, vinegar, a pot for boiling water.

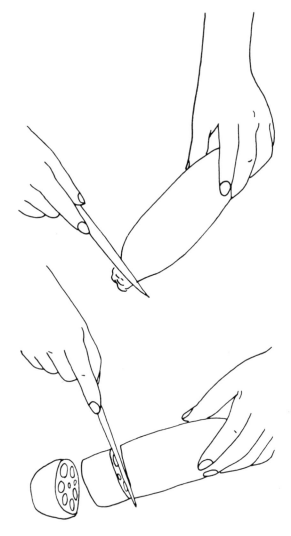

1. Cut a 2-inch section from a lotus root.

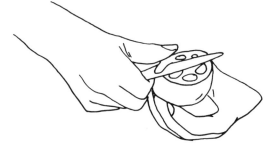

2. Shape in the form of a ball.

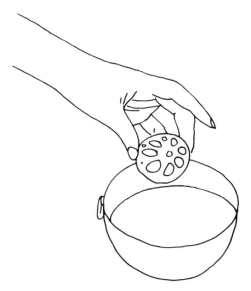

3. Soak immediately for 2 minutes in a solution of Fruit-Fresh (mix 2 tablespoons per cup of water) to prevent browning. When you have cut enough balls, cook in slightly vinegared water until just done.

LOTUS ARROW

The trick to this garnish is slicing the lotus root on a strong diagonal. When it is subsequently cut and put together with the grooves upward, they will be angled in an arrowlike way. We hope it will point you to a long and pleasant association with Mukimono. See color plate 36.

SERVING SUGGESTIONS: Use to garnish a buffet.

YOU WILL NEED: lotus root, knife, Fruit-Fresh, vinegar, a pot for boiling water, toothpick.

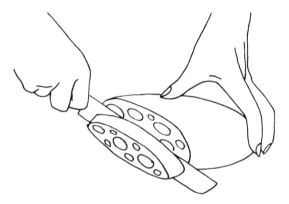

1. Cut a ¾-inch slice of lotus root on the diagonal as shown.

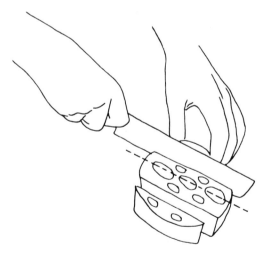

2. Cut a 1-inch section from the center. Try to line up two or three holes along the centerline of this piece.

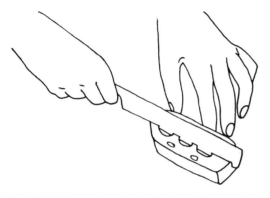

3. Cut this section in half along the centerline.

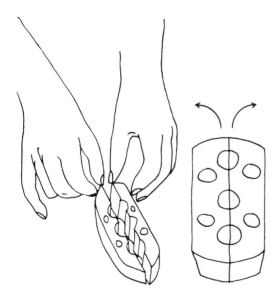

4. Turn each half outward.

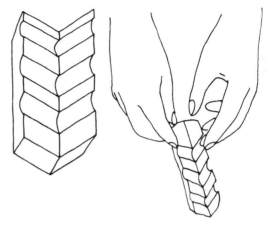

5. Bring them together, as shown. This will create the arrowlike diagonal grooves. Temporarily secure the two halves with a toothpick. Be sure to remove the toothpick before serving.

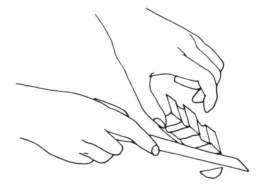

6. Trim in the shape of an arrowpoint. Soak in Fruit-Fresh (mix 2 tablespoons per cup of water) immediately. When enough are made, boil in lightly vinegared water until just done.

SOME
SIMPLE
DISHES

37. CHAWAN MUSHI
(p. 81)

38. ACORN SQUASH
WITH GOMA MISO
(p. 87)

39. ROLLED NAMBAN BEEF (p. 91)

40. SHRIMP AND CUCUMBER WITH KIMIZU (p. 97)

41. LEEK WITH SUMISO
(p. 103)

42. SCALLOPS WITH
SHŌGA SAUCE
(p. 106)

43. KIJIYAKI DONBURI
(p. 110)

44. TOFU ANKAKE
(p. 115)

We have decided to conclude the book with some simple Japanese dishes, several of which could be incorporated nicely into Western dinners as first courses. Others, such as Kijiyaki Donburi, make for a tasty lunch or light dinner. In all cases, we have tried to show how to present the food attractively. Presentation has always been an important part of Japanese cuisine and adds immeasurably to the enjoyment of a meal.

What should be obvious from the start is that the Japanese don't feel obliged to use our conventional Western round dinner plate. They use an infinite variety of dishes, cups, and bowls in pottery, porcelain, and lacquerware. There is great tradition here, which unfortunately goes beyond the scope of this book. But at the very least, we would like to urge you to experiment. It's lots of fun and, believe it or not, the food really will taste special.

Since certain ingredients called for in the recipes might be unfamiliar, we have prepared short descriptions. These foods should be available in most Oriental markets.

Dashi. The basic soup stock used by all Japanese chefs, dashi is made by preparing a broth from konbu (dried kelp) and shavings of katsuo bushi (dried bonito). Instant dashi that dissolves in hot water is also available. If dashi cannot be found, chicken stock may be used, but, of course, there is no comparison.

Ginger Root. This is the spicy root of the ginger plant. The fresh root can be found in many Western, as well as Oriental, markets. Although it is available in powdered form, it is the fresh root that we are after. When buying ginger root look for firm ones; soft, mushy spots will indicate deterioration. Ginger juice is made by cutting off a piece of the root and squeezing it in a press, such as a garlic press.

Mirin. Mirin is a heavy, sweet sake. It contains about 13 percent alcohol and is used exclusively for cooking, so you should look for it in Oriental markets rather than liquor stores.

Miso. This is a fermented soybean paste. Since miso is becoming quite well known in America, you should have no trouble locating it. Generally speaking, all miso is made by injecting boiled soybeans with an activating mold (koji) and allowing it to ferment for as much as three years. Although there are myriad varieties of miso, the broad division (like wine) is into red and white. We are using red miso in these recipes. It will be identified as such on the label. Most red miso requires lengthy ageing to achieve its coloration.

Mustard (Karashi). This is a Japanese dry mustard. If it is hard to find, the spice section of your supermarket will contain a half-dozen other varieties. We are using Coleman's dry mustard. The spiciness in powdered mustard is created when it is mixed with water and made into a paste. It should be allowed to stand covered for about 10 minutes to fully develop its flavor.

Rice Vinegar (Su). Rice vinegar is made from naturally fermented rice. It is a mild, slightly sweet vinegar, unlike sharper Western varieties. After heating it does not lose its vinegar flavor and tartness. Japanese rice vinegar is usually white. There is a red rice vinegar, but it is a select product made only for special sushi shops in Tokyo. White rice vinegar can be bought by the bottle in Oriental markets or large chain supermarkets.

Sake. Sake is the comparatively inexpensive Japanese rice wine and is usually available in wine and liquor stores. It is fairly strong, about 19 percent alcohol. Japanese chefs sometimes ignite the sake before using it to allow this alcohol to burn off. As a beverage it can be served either warm or cold. Sake is one of the main flavoring ingredients in Japanese cuisine.

Sansho Powder. Unfortunately, sansho powder is probably going to be difficult to find in some areas. It is the ground pod of the sansho tree and is used like pepper over chicken and fish.

Sesame Seeds. These seeds come from the pod of the sesame plant. They are always toasted. Also, you may grind them into a paste about the consistency of peanut butter. Both black and white sesame seeds are available. The choice usually depends on the color accent desired rather than taste.

Sesame Seed Oil. This is the rather strongly flavored oil derived from the sesame seed. It is used primarily for flavoring, and is not a cooking oil.

Shiitake Mushroom. These mushrooms are cultivated on the bark of the shii-tree and other oak-related species. They are being cultivated in California now and so should be readily available. They can be purchased either fresh or dried.

Soy Sauce (Shoyu). Soy sauce is a salty brown sauce made by naturally fermenting soybeans, wheat, and salt. It is probably the best known of all Japanese seasonings in America. Soy sauce comes in both light and dark varieties. Generally, the light is used to preserve the color of lighter foods. A mild soy sauce that has some of the salt extracted (reduced from 14.9 percent to 8.8 percent) is also manufactured.

Tofu. Tofu is one of the "big three" products that Asia has learned to create from the soybean. (Miso and shoyu are the other two.) Soy milk is coagulated to create curds, which are poured into rectangular molds for shaping. In Japan and in some parts of the United States, tofu is sold in small cakes that are cut from these large blocks floating in water. Most American supermarkets sell tofu packed in water in small sealed plastic tubs. These are date-stamped and should be used within one week of the manufacturing date. Tofu should always be kept floating in water and refrigerated. The water should be changed daily. Nowadays, Japanese grocery stores sell a tofu kit that contains instant tofu, a mold, and a solidifying agent.

CHAWAN MUSHI

Chawan Mushi makes a surprisingly delightful, although somewhat unconventional, soup course, since the egg custard sets completely during steaming. Enough of the rich juices are released, however, to give it something of a liquid quality.

The Japanese serve this dish hot in the winter and chilled in the summer. We are using traditional Chawan Mushi bowls with covers, but any small deep bowl will do if you do not have these. Even a mug would be a good choice if you are serving it as part of a light lunch. See color plate 37.

INGREDIENTS

½ chicken breast
4 shrimp
2 dried shiitake mushrooms

CUSTARD
3 eggs
3 cups chicken stock
2 teaspoons light soy sauce
2 teaspoons mirin
1 teaspoon salt

4 parsley stems

Serves 4

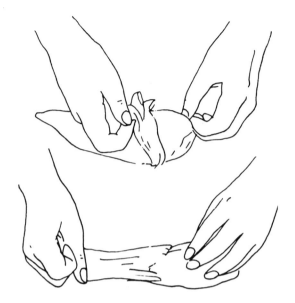

1. Bone and remove skin from ½ chicken breast.

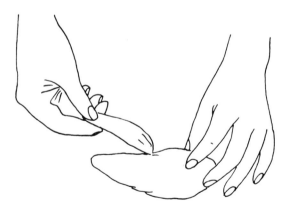

2. Separate the filet from the breast. For this recipe, only the filet will be used.

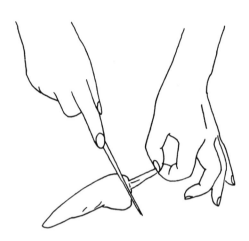

3. Pull sinews from filet.

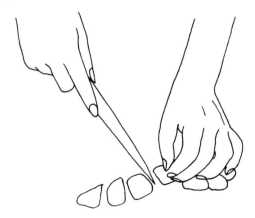

4. Cut into eight pieces.

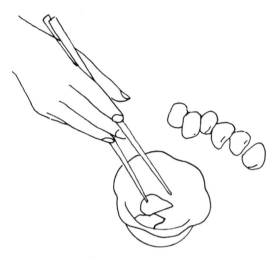

5. Place two pieces in the bottom of each serving cup.

7. Soak mushrooms in tepid water until soft, about 20 minutes.

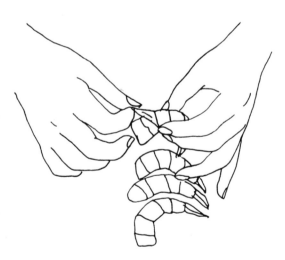

6. Shell and devein shrimp, leaving tails intact.

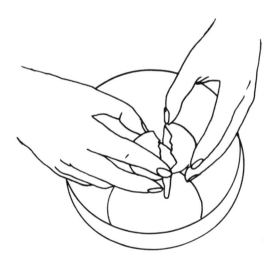

8. Break eggs into mixing bowl.

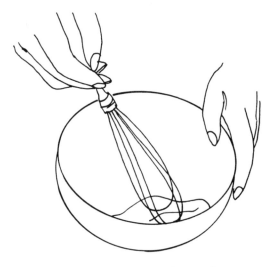

9. Beat eggs lightly by hand. (We do not want to create too many bubbles.) Add remaining custard ingredients. Stir lightly.

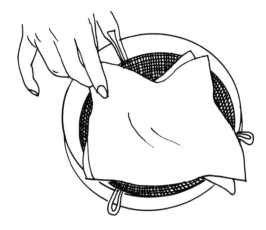

10. Line sieve with two thicknesses of cheesecloth.

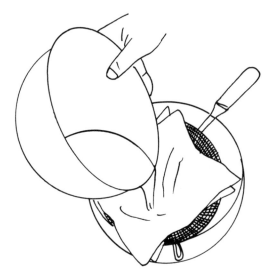

11. Strain custard mixture through cheesecloth.

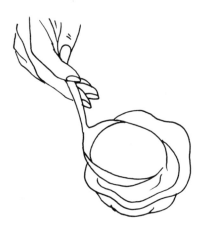

12. Ladle mixture into individual cups to about ½ inch from the top.

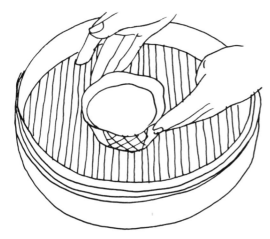

13. Place in a hot steamer. We are using a bamboo steamer, but Western metal ones are fine.

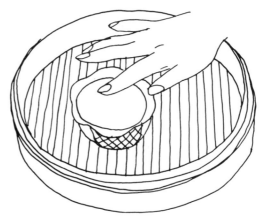

15. Steam over medium-low heat for about 10 to 13 minutes, depending on the depth of the cup. A shallow cup will require less time. To test, remove cover and press lightly with fingertip to check firmness.

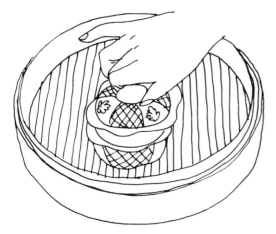

14. Cover the cup with its own lid, or cover tightly with foil if lid is not available. Cover the steamer.

16. When custard has just begun to set add shrimp. Cut off stem and squeeze excess water from the shiitake mushrooms. Quarter and add two pieces to each cup. Cover again and steam for 3 to 4 minutes more. Do not overcook or holes will appear and custard will toughen.

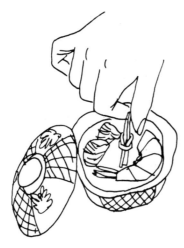

17. Remove from steamer and add garnish (Carrot Knot, p. 4. Note: We are using a parsley stem instead of a carrot for this garnish).

ACORN SQUASH
WITH GOMA MISO

The body's protein requirements are well known. Protein is so essential to the cells of all living matter that no life can exist without it. Twenty-two amino acids make up the proteins in our bodies. Fourteen of these can be synthesized within the body. Eight cannot and must be supplied by the diet. These eight are known as essential protein. Miso contains these eight and is considered a source of complete high-quality protein. Here we are using it in combination with sesame seeds to create a tasty sauce for acorn squash. See color plate 38.

INGREDIENTS

1 small acorn squash
3½ tablespoons white sesame seeds

MISO SAUCE
4 tablespoons miso
1½ tablespoons mirin
2 tablespoons sugar
5 tablespoons dashi or chicken stock

Serves 4

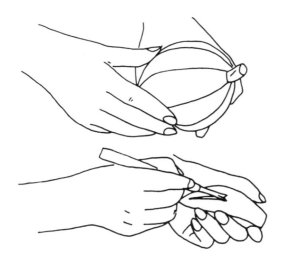

1. Select a small acorn squash with 12 or more ridges. Prepare 12 Acorn Squash Leaf garnishes (p. 68).

2. Place the sections in a steamer and steam until just done. Try to arrange in one layer only.

3. Heat a small frying pan over high heat. When a drop of water flicked on its surface evaporates instantly, add 3½ tablespoons of sesame seeds and turn heat down to low. Toast while shaking the pan constantly. When two or three seeds start to pop, take the pan off the heat and squash a few seeds between your thumb and forefinger. They are done when they give off a toasty aroma. It is very easy to overroast the seeds and lose their flavor, so be attentive.

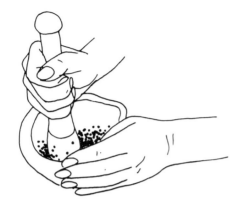

4. Immediately empty the seeds into a mortar and grind until slightly oily. Set aside.

6. Remove from the heat and add ground sesame seeds.

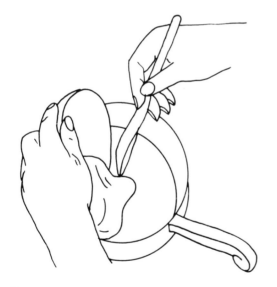

5. Combine Miso Sauce ingredients in a small saucepan. Cook over low heat until the sauce becomes smooth and shiny.

7. Mix thoroughly.

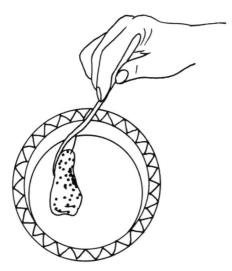

8. Spoon a small amount of sauce into each individual serving bowl.

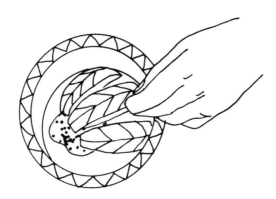

9. Arrange the squash attractively in the bowls, and serve.

ROLLED NAMBAN BEEF

In the period before the closing of Japan (1603) the countries of Southeast Asia were known as Namban. Portuguese and Spanish explorers who arrived in Japan via these countries were called Namban jin. These individuals brought with them a taste for deep-fried foods, onions, and peppers. This kind of culinary adventurism was unknown in Japan at the time, and all such foods were labeled Namban or Southern barbarian. See color plate 39.

INGREDIENTS

4 slices boneless rib steak, ¼ inch thick
8 large scallions
1 tablespoon Japanese-style sesame seed oil
1 cup flour
Oil for deep-frying

MARINADE
2 teaspoons ginger, sliced paper-thin
½ teaspoon dried crushed red pepper
3½ teaspoons rice vinegar
3 tablespoons sugar
3 tablespoons dark soy sauce
2 tablespoons sake

Serves 4

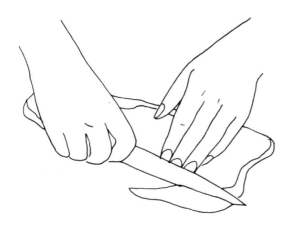

1. Trim fat from beef slices.

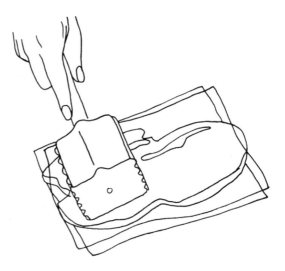

3. Pound until very thin.

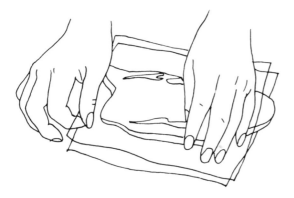

2. Place each beef slice between two sheets of waxed paper.

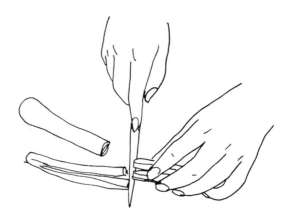

4. Cut off the white of the scallions. Cut the greens to match them in length. Discard the short remainders.

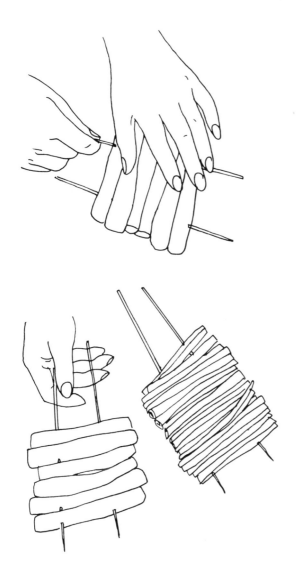

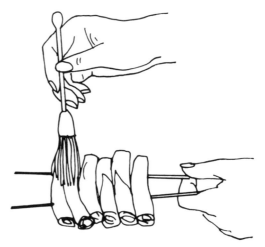

6. Brush scallions with sesame seed oil.

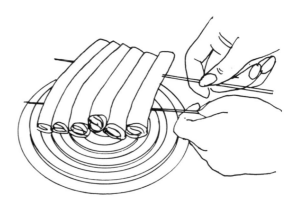

7. Toast scallions over burner until slightly brown.

5. Using thin metal skewers, skewer scallion whites and greens separately, as shown.

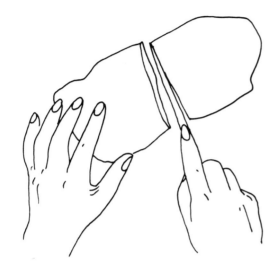

8. Cut beef slices in half.

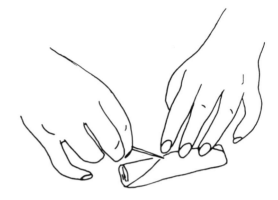

10. Secure with a toothpick.

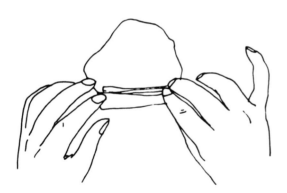

9. Put one scallion white and a few greens on the cut edge of the beef and roll it up.

11. Roll in flour.

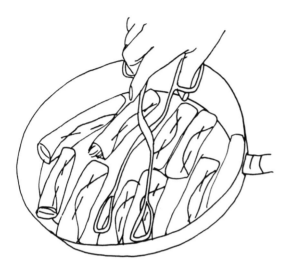

12. Heat oil. Deep-fry the beef until golden brown.

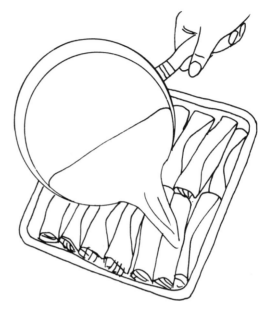

14. Place beef in deep pan, preferably in one layer. Pour hot marinade over beef. It is important for both marinade and beef to be hot to ensure that marinade flavor soaks into beef. Marinate for about 20 minutes, turning several times.

13. While beef is frying, combine marinade ingredients and cook over medium heat.

15. Cut into bite-size pieces.

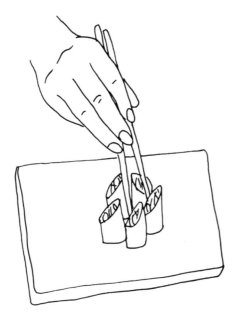

16. Place on dish with garnish (Tomato Dahlia, p. 60).

SHRIMP AND CUCUMBER WITH KIMIZU

Japanese food design usually requires small portions and exquisite presentation. Many dishes, therefore, fit rather nicely into the Western dinner as first courses. And so it is with this shrimp dish. See color plate 40.

INGREDIENTS

12 large shrimp
1 tablespoon lemon juice
1 cucumber
½ teaspoon salt

KIMIZU DRESSING
2 eggs
1 tablespoon sugar
⅓ teaspoon salt
2 teaspoons mirin
3 tablespoons lemon juice
2 tablespoons dashi
1 teaspoon light soy sauce

Serves 4

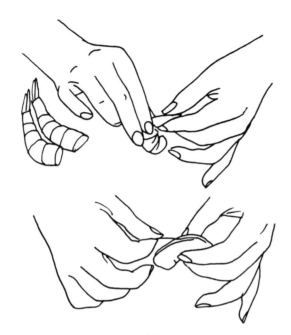

1. Shell and devein shrimp.

3. Put 1 tablespoon lemon juice in 2 cups of boiling water.

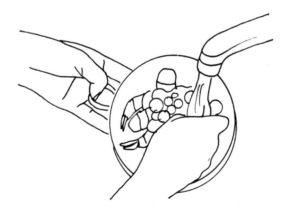

2. Wash gently in cold water and drain.

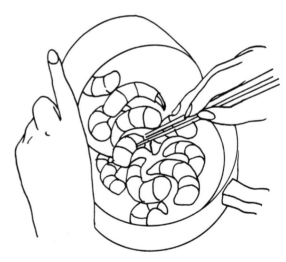

4. Add shrimp and boil until just pink, about 2 minutes.

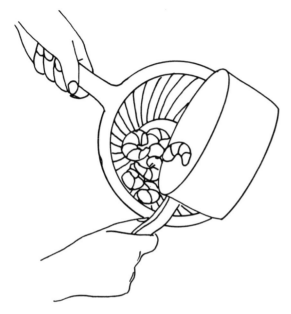

5. Drain.

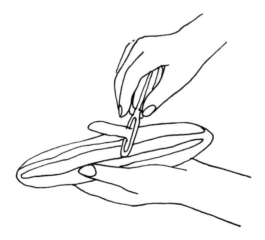

6. Peel the cucumber, leaving strips of skin for pattern.

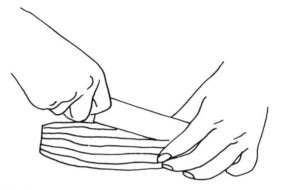

7. Cut in half lengthwise.

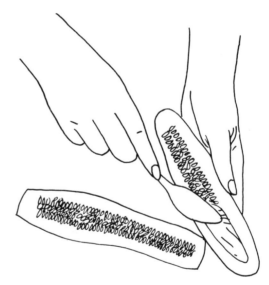

8. Remove seeds.

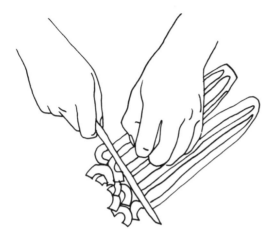

9. Cut in paper-thin slices.

11. Squeeze cucumbers with your hands to eliminate excess water.

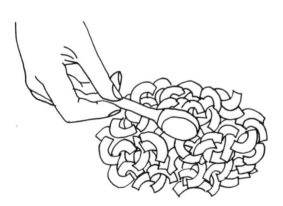

10. Spread out on cutting board and sprinkle with ½ teaspoon salt. Let sit for about 1 minute, or until crispiness is lost.

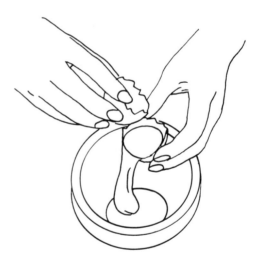

12. Separate 2 eggs.

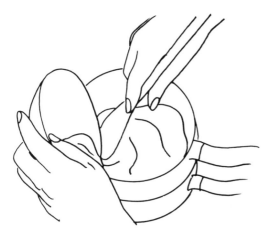

13. Beat egg yolks lightly in the top of a double boiler. Add the rest of the Kimizu Dressing ingredients, and stir over boiling water until the mixture becomes thick and creamy. Stir sauce constantly while cooking to ensure smooth texture. Remove from boiling water and cool to room temperature.

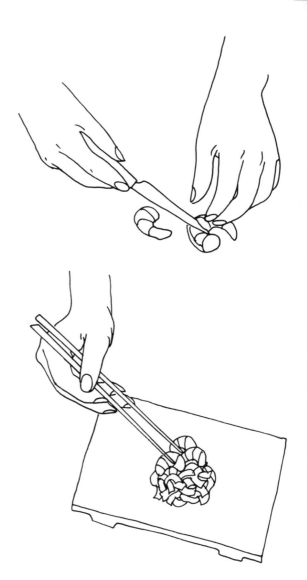

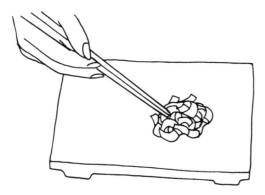

14. Place cucumber on plates.

15. Cut shrimp in half. Place on plate.

16. Spoon sauce over shrimp and cucumber, and add garnish (Jaws, p. 22).

LEEK WITH SUMISO

INGREDIENTS

8 small leeks
2 teaspoons salad oil
A pinch of salt

SUMISO SAUCE
¼ cup red miso
2 tablespoons sugar
1½ tablespoons dashi
1 tablespoon lemon juice

Serves 4

It is estimated that 85 percent of the total annual production of miso in Japan is used in miso soup. For the Japanese, it replaces the morning cup of coffee. But unlike coffee it is abundantly rich in essential nutrients and offers lasting energy throughout the morning. In this recipe we are using miso as a sauce, in order to appreciate its rich flavor. See color plate 41.

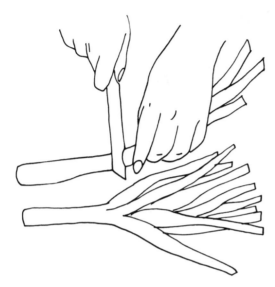

1. Cut the white section from leeks.

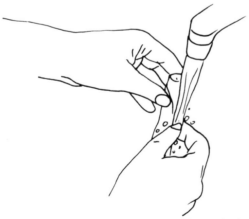

2. Wash thoroughly under cold running water. Leeks trap a lot of sand and it must be removed.

3. Poach leeks in boiling water until just done. Drain.

4. Brush with oil, and sprinkle with a pinch of salt. Set aside.

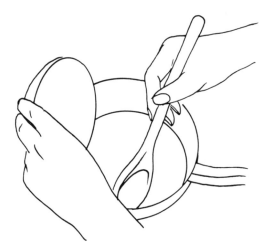

5. In a small saucepan combine sauce ingredients (except lemon juice). Cook over medium heat while stirring, until sauce becomes smooth and shiny. The shininess occurs when the sugar melts. Remove from heat. Add lemon juice and mix thoroughly.

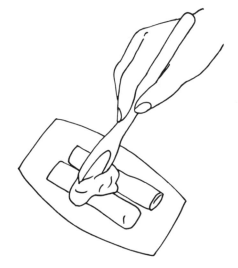

7. Spoon on small quantity of sauce.

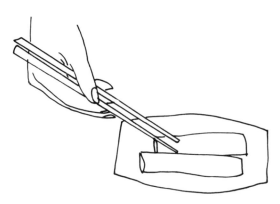

6. Place leeks on serving plates.

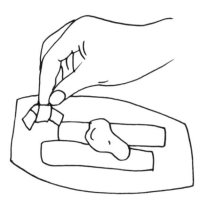

8. Add garnish (Carrot Tie, p. 6).

SCALLOPS WITH SHŌGA SAUCE

In Sandro Botticelli's painting *The Birth of Venus* we see the classical goddess standing lightly on a shell that is being blown ashore amid a shower of roses. In college art classes we irreverently referred to this famous work as "Venus on the Half-shell," which implies an oyster shell. In truth, she is being borne on a giant scallop shell. The scallop is found in all of the seas of the world. In Japan they are abundant in the Hokkaido area. We usually eat only the white, sweet adductor muscle, although the surrounding darker mantle is also edible. See color plate 42.

INGREDIENTS

20 scallops
1 cup cornstarch
3 tablespoons cooking oil

SHŌGA SAUCE
1 tablespoon light soy sauce
2 tablespoons sake
2 tablespoons mirin
1 teaspoon sugar
¼ teaspoon ginger juice
⅓ cup dashi
½ cup water
1½ teaspoons cornstarch

Serves 4

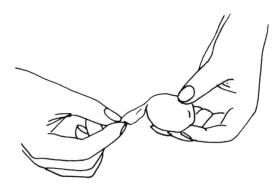

1. Pull off the small tough section of the scallops.

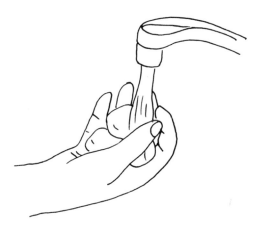

2. Wash thoroughly under cold water and drain well.

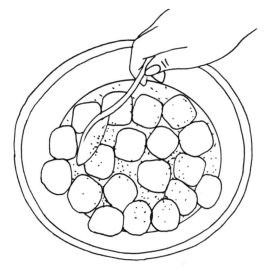

3. Put 1 cup of cornstarch in a large plate. Dredge scallops.

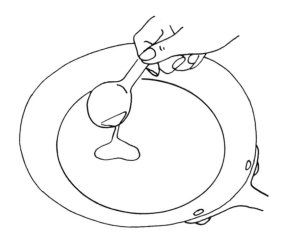

4. Heat the oil in a large frying pan over medium heat.

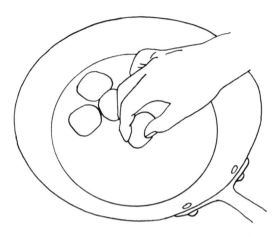

5. Dust off excess cornstarch and gently place scallops in pan to cook. Fry for 2 minutes and carefully turn them over.

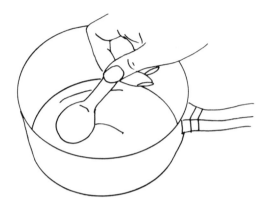

7. Put sauce ingredients (except cornstarch) into a small saucepan and cook over low heat until sauce reduces to ⅓ cup.

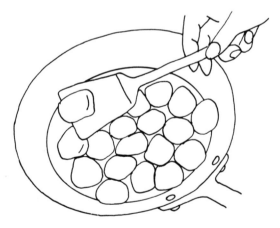

6. Fry for 2 or 3 minutes longer. Do not overcook, as it will cause toughness.

8. Combine 1½ teaspoons cornstarch and 1 tablespoon water in a small cup. Mix thoroughly. While stirring, pour a third of the hot sauce into the cup. Continue to stir.

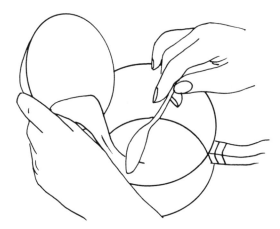

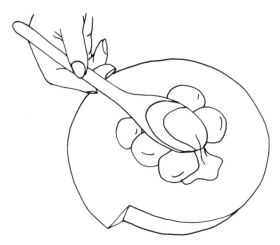

9. Pour this mixture back into saucepan and stir constantly over low heat until sauce becomes transparent and thickens. Set aside.

11. Spoon sauce over the scallops. Add garnish (Pine Tree, p. 26).

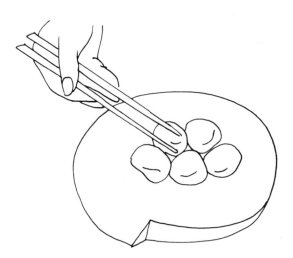

10. Place scallops on individual serving plates.

KIJIYAKI DONBURI

It would hardly be proper to present even as few as eight recipes without including at least one rice dish. The word *donburi* is usually used to indicate a deep bowl of rice with either meat, fish, egg, or vegetable topping. Unagi Donburi, for example, is a bowl of rice topped with broiled eel. Actually, the topping for a donburi can be almost anything. *Kijiyaki* really means wild pheasant, but because of the scarcity of pheasant (it is illegal to hunt them in Japan), chicken has often been used as a substitute in this recipe, although the name kijiyaki still sticks. See color plate 43.

INGREDIENTS

2 cups rice
2 whole chicken breasts

MARINADE
½ cup soy sauce
¼ cup sake

2 small green peppers
4 tablespoons cooking oil

KIJIYAKI SAUCE
½ cup water
¼ cup mirin
3 tablespoons soy sauce
1 tablespoon sugar
2 teaspoons minced ginger root

½ teaspoon salt
¼ teaspoon sansho powder (if available)

Serves 4

1. Steam rice. A Japanese automatic rice cooker is a great help in this task.

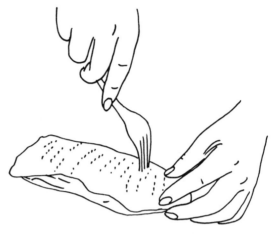

3. Prick skin side all over with fork. This will keep the skin from shrinking and will allow the marinade to penetrate.

2. Cut chicken breasts in half and bone.

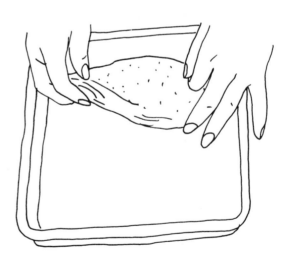

4. Place the breasts in a shallow pan.

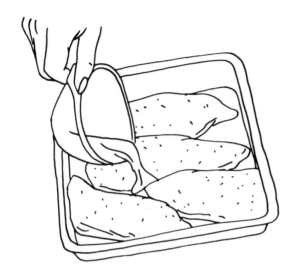

5. Mix marinade and pour over breasts.

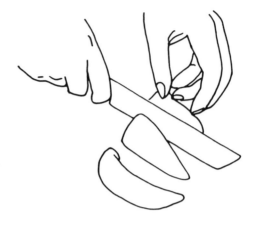

7. Cut each half into thirds.

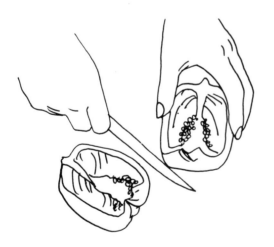

6. While chicken is marinating, cut the green peppers in half and remove the seeds.

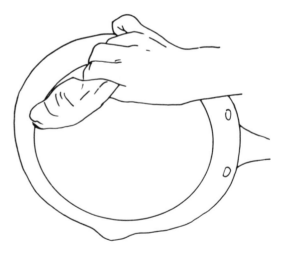

8. Place a large skillet over high heat. Add 3 tablespoons oil. When oil is heated place chicken skin side down in one layer. Fry until skin turns golden brown.

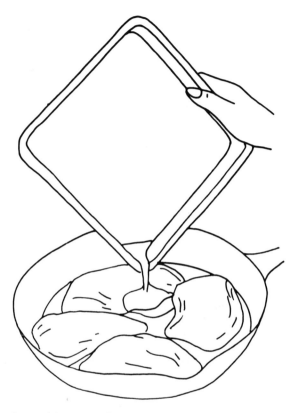

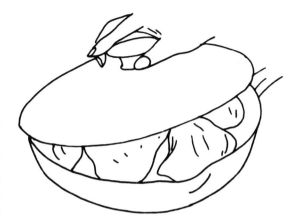

11. Cover and turn heat down to low. Cook for 10 to 12 minutes, turning once for even cooking.

9. Add marinade.

10. Combine ingredients for Kijiyaki Sauce and add to skillet.

12. Remove chicken and set aside. Turn heat up and bring liquid to a boil. Boil until sauce thickens slightly.

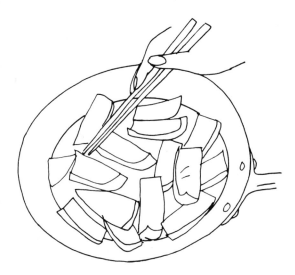

13. Place remaining tablespoon of oil into another frying pan over high heat. Put green peppers in and sauté until just done. Sprinkle with salt.

15. Put steamed rice into individual serving bowls and top with chicken slices. Add green peppers. Spoon sauce over chicken and peppers. If sansho powder is available, sprinkle over top of chicken. Add garnish (Carrot Butterfly, p. 16).

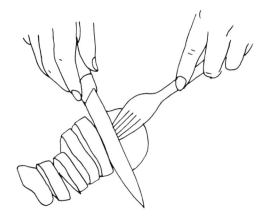

14. Slice chicken breasts into bite-size pieces.

TOFU ANKAKE

Tofu can be prepared in an almost un-limited variety of ways, even in tofu-burgers. But for this recipe, we have chosen one of its simpler versions to preserve the basic tofu taste. See color plate 44.

INGREDIENTS

Approximately 4 ounces Japanese
    soft tofu

ANKAKE SAUCE
½ cup chicken stock
⅓ cup sake
2 tablespoons soy sauce
1½ tablespoons cornstarch

1 tablespoon dry mustard

Serves 4

115

2. Slice four small rectangular pieces from the block. If you have tofu left over, place it in a covered bowl of cold water and refrigerate. Change water daily. Do not consume after date stamped on container.

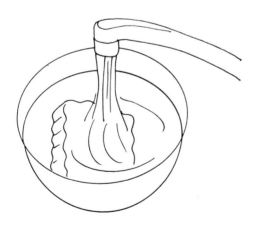

1. Remove the tofu from its package and rinse gently with cold water.

3. Gently place the pieces in boiling water. Turn the heat down and simmer until just done. Do not let the water come to a boil.

4. Combine Ankake Sauce ingredients (except cornstarch) in a saucepan, and heat until almost boiling. Reduce heat to medium.

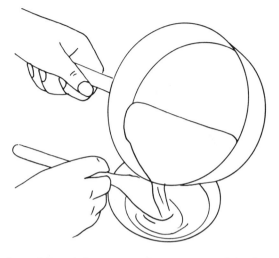

6. While stirring, pour about ¼ cup of the hot sauce into the cornstarch. Pour this mixture back into the sauce and cook, stirring constantly until the sauce thickens.

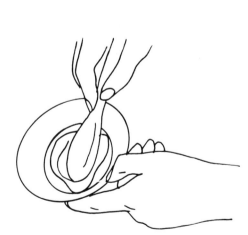

5. Mix cornstarch with 1 tablespoon of water and stir thoroughly.

7. Use a slotted spoon to scoop tofu gently out of hot water, and place in serving bowls.

8. Ladle hot sauce over tofu until it's almost covered.

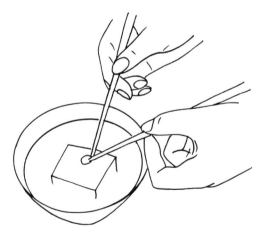

9. Mix powdered mustard with a little hot water to make a paste. Dot the center of the tofu with mustard. Place extra mustard on the side in a Wasabi Boat (p. 24).